# LAS VEGAS
## and
# LAUGHLIN, NEVADA

## Automobile Club of Southern California

Cover photo:
*The Egyptian-themed Luxor Las Vegas hotel-casino.*

Although information presented in this publication has been carefully researched and was as accurate as possible at press time, the Automobile Club of Southern California is not responsible for any changes or errors which may occur. It is wise to verify information immediately prior to your visit.

Only attractions or establishments that are approved by an Automobile Club of Southern California field representative may advertise. The purchase of advertising, however, has no effect on inspections and evaluations. Advertisements provide the reader with additional information which may be useful in selecting what to see and where to stay.

Additional advertisements (excluding attractions and establishments) for travel-related services may also be included in ACSC publications. Acceptance of these advertisements does not imply endorsement by ACSC.

**ISBN: 1-56413-422-9**
Printed in the United States of America

# Table of Contents

# LAS VEGAS &
# LAUGHLIN, NEVADA

*Southern Nevada is a land of extremes and contrasts: mega-resorts and huge dams, the spectacle of bizarre rock formations and the din of gambling halls, dressed-up showgirls and fuzzy burros, thrill rides and wedding chapels.... People love it and hate it, sometimes all at once. But from the barren desert to the most elaborate casinos and hotels, Southern Nevada and all its offerings cannot be ignored.*

*L*as Vegas is one of the nation's favorite vacation destinations. It's a 24-hour city where gambling reigns supreme and dreams of striking it rich sometime come true. But Las Vegas has many facets, and casino action is just one of them. It also offers luxurious resort lodgings, top-name entertainment, inexpensive dining, world-class golf courses, scenic desert treks, nearby water recreation, and most recently, plenty of activities for children. Las Vegas is home to nine of the 10 largest resort hotels in the world—top of the list being the 5005-room MGM Grand Hotel Casino & Theme Park. Not surprisingly, there are also more hotel rooms here than any other city in the U.S.: 105,000, with thousands more on the way. In 1997 Las Vegas attracted an estimated 31 million visitors, up more than 5 percent from 1996 and a figure that just seems to keep growing.

*L*aughlin, by contrast, offers a more relaxed atmosphere than its flashy, northern counterpart. It is an oasis along the Colorado River, where the state lines of California, Nevada and Arizona merge. Like its famous neighbor, Laughlin offers plenty of gaming action, but the river remains one of its strongest assets. The area, which generally includes adjacent **Bullhead City, Arizona**, has long been known as a haven for "snowbirds" in winter (travelers from cold climes who migrate during the winter to the sun-belt states) and the river crowd in summer. Boating, fishing, water-skiing and swimming in the river's surprisingly frigid waters are favorite pursuits of vacationers, especially during the sizzling heat of summer (capable of frying eggs on a sidewalk). Combine the lure of the river with reasonably priced rooms, countless buffets, and even an

*Theme hotels dominate the new Las Vegas Strip.*

*Laughlin has become a boomtown on the banks of the Colorado River.*

international airport, and it should be no surprise that Laughlin has gained such a foothold in the West. In 1996, more than 4.6 million tourists visited this small desert community.

*A*nother town quickly making a name for itself is tiny **Primm**, located along I-15 40 miles south of Las Vegas at the California-Nevada border. Once just a meager drive-through known as Stateline, the settlement now boasts the world's tallest and fastest roller coaster, the "Desperado," and is the site of three large resort-style hotels, a 6500-seat arena, a monorail and various other attractions.

## Climate

Las Vegas experiences about 294 days of sunshine per year and an average high temperature of 79 degrees Fahrenheit. This high desert community has an arid climate, low humidity and a yearly rainfall of about 4.13 inches. Spring and fall generally bring the mildest weather, when daytime highs are in the comfortable 70-degree range. Winter months, by contrast, can be

quite cool, with highs in the 50s and lows in the 30s.

At the peak of summer, the temperature often climbs above 100 degrees. But the heat is easily escaped via air conditioning, swimming pools or jaunts to water parks. Scenic Mount Charleston in the Spring Mountains National Recreation Area also offers a break from the heat with its cooler upper elevation temperatures.

Laughlin is located on the northeast edge of the Mojave Desert and has a high mean temperature of about 87 degrees. In this hot, dry region, the summer months routinely sizzle above the 100-degree mark, sometimes climbing above 120 degrees. But relief is always close at hand in the form of air conditioning and the frigid water of the Colorado River. Sometimes higher-than-average humidity triggers summer thunderstorms and flash floods, turning the area's dry washes into turbulent rivers. Winters can be equally severe with below freezing temperatures. Rainfall averages about 4 inches a year.

INDIAN SPRINGS

NEVADA

GLENDALE

95

93

15

VALLEY OF FIRE
STATE
PARK

*Virgin River*

SPRING
MOUNTAINS
NATIONAL
RECREATION
AREA

RED ROCK

CANYON

★ LAS VEGAS

515

*Lake
Mead*

*Colorado River*

NATIONAL

CONS.

93
95

△ AREA
*Potosi Mtn.*

HENDERSON

BOULDER
CITY

LAKE MEAD
HOOVER
DAM

NATIONAL

RECREATION

AREA

15

95

PRIMM

164

CALIFORNIA

*Colorado*

*Lake
Mohave*

93

AUTOMOBILE CLUB
SOUTHERN CALIFORNIA
AAA

N
W    E
S

163

68

LAUGHLIN ★

DAVIS DAM

BULLHEAD CITY

KINGMAN

OATMAN

40

40

227

NEEDLES

66

ARIZONA

*River*

LAKE HAVASU
CITY

95

95

*Lake Havasu*

PARKER DAM

62

PARKER

LAS VEGAS and
LAUGHLIN, NEVADA

SCALE IN MILES

0   5   10   15   20   25

MAP 2772

## ▼ Showing the Way

To guide travelers through the area's varied and sometimes staggering array of attractions, the Automobile Club of Southern California created this book as a reference to the many activities, points of interest and places to stay in Las Vegas, Laughlin and surrounding areas. In addition to *Las Vegas and Laughlin, Nevada,* the Auto Club produces a number of companion publications. The *Guide to Colorado River* covers the river area from Lake Mead to Yuma, and provides thorough map coverage and information on recreation and local attractions. Publications covering nearby areas include the *Explore! San Bernardino County* map, which offers a recreation guide, listings for points of interest and detailed maps; and the *California Desert Areas* book, a retail publication which provides extensive information on tourist and recreational activities and events, lodging, dining and camping listings, as well as area history and other related topics, all presented in full color. These publications are available to AAA members at Auto Club district offices, as well as to nonmembers at selected Central and Southern California booksellers.

# Activities For Children

Because Las Vegas and Laughlin are usually considered adult-oriented cities, visitors in the past have often left children at home. Today, however, both desert communities offer many daytime diversions for the younger set. Nearly all of the larger hotels have video arcades on the premises and some even offer supervised children's programs.

In Las Vegas, the MGM Grand is the home of **King Looey's Youth Center**, a four-room facility that has supervised activities for children ages 3 to 16. Arts and crafts, air hockey, basketball, group games and preschool activities are featured, and food service is available. The center also offers daily supervised excursions to the hotel's **theme park** for ages 6 to 16. Reservations are strongly advised. The 33-acre attraction features roller coasters and water rides, bumper cars and musical acts.

Boulder Station is another hotel/casino that provides comprehensive child-care services. Its new **Kids Quest** play area offers supervised care for children from six weeks to 12 years old. The 8000-square-foot facility includes a huge play structure with slides, tubes and tunnels, a big-screen video room, kid's karaoke, Barbie Land, a shadow wall, arcade games and a "tiny tot" room for children up to 30 months old. Reservations are advised, especially on weekends. Additional child-care services in Las Vegas can be found by referring to the telephone directory yellow pages under "Baby Sitters."

As for the main youth attractions (although adults seem to like them just as much), the Circus Circus Hotel has several shops and food stands catering to children. The second floor boasts a **carnival-style arcade** and free **circus acts.**

**Grand Slam Canyon Adventuredome**, adjacent to Circus Circus, is a five-acre, climate-controlled indoor amusement park. The attractions include a water flume ride with a 60-foot free fall and the nation's only double-loop, double-corkscrew indoor roller coaster.

The Excalibur Hotel delights young children with its medieval castle-theme exterior and Renaissance village interior. **Strolling performers, carnival-style**

*Rafting on the Colorado River is just one of many recreational activities available in the Las Vegas region.*

**arcade games** and a nightly **jousting tournament** can all be found here. Excalibur also has **Merlin's Magic Motion Machine,** a dynamic motion simulator that provides filmed "rides" for passengers whose seats are programmed to move with the motion on the screen.

Excalibur's Egyptian neighbor is the pyramid-shaped Luxor, which features an eclectic mix of **Egyptian replicas,** including an enormous **sphinx** in front and a **full-size reproduction of King Tut's tomb**. Other enticing distractions are a **video arcade** and a series of **motion simulated films**.

Still more fun and games can be found in the Coney Island Emporium at New York New York Hotel & Casino. The emporium features **midway-style carnival games; laser tag; an eight-player, Daytona-style, interactive driving simulator; bumper cars; shooting galleries** and more. Next door to the emporium is the Manhattan Express **roller coaster,** nearly a mile in length with a maximum drop of 144 feet.

A spectacular five-story **waterfall** and **volcano** are located at the entrance to The Mirage. Every night the manmade volcano erupts in a dramatic fashion, spewing fire and smoke—and stopping traffic on Las Vegas Boulevard. Dramatic night lighting makes the waterfall appear to be flowing lava. Inside the hotel, children will enjoy the **Dolphin and Secret Garden Habitat** or the **white tiger display**.

Treasure Island, next to The Mirage, features a spectacular **pirate show** several times nightly. Live actors, dressed in swashbuckling gear, battle it out right in front of the hotel on Las Vegas Boulevard. Dazzling, fiery explosions and even the sinking of a ship provide exciting entertainment for all ages.

Then there's GameWorks, a huge virtual-reality arcade that opened in 1997, with **almost 300 video games of all description**. The centerpiece is Surge Rock, at 75 feet **one of the world's tallest free-standing rock-climbing structures**. Crowds gather to watch climbers of all

*The 1950s-themed shop at the Everything Coca-Cola store sells merchandise celebrating the venerable soft drink.*

Other highlights for children include visits to the **"Desperado"** roller coaster and other thrill rides in Primm, while Henderson touts the **Cranberry World West, Ethel M Chocolates Factory, Ron Lee's World of Clowns** and **Favorite Brands Marshmallow Factory**.

Las Vegas, meanwhile, has many more venues for young people, including the **Guinness World of Records Museum, Imperial Palace Auto Collection, Las Vegas Museum of Natural History, Las Vegas Mini Grand Prix, Lied Discovery Children's Museum, Magic & Movie Hall of Fame, Nevada State Museum and Historical Society, Scandia Family Fun Center, Southern Nevada Zoological-Botanical Park, Wet 'N Wild** and **World of Coca-Cola Las Vegas**. Details about these attractions can be found in the *Las Vegas Valley, Outside Las Vegas* and *Laughlin-Bullhead City* chapters.

While Laughlin's orientation toward gambling is geared mostly to adults, parents will find plenty of activities to entertain their children in and around the gambling center.

The Colorado Belle, Edgewater, Flamingo Hilton, Gold River, Harrah's Laughlin, Pioneer, Ramada Express and Riverside hotels all have **video arcades**. First-run **movies** are shown at Don Laughlin's Riverside Resort Hotel and at theaters in Bullhead City. **Boat trips** on the Colorado River offer both fresh air and adventure.

ages try their luck at scaling the earth-tone rock.

For a total change of environment, **Valley of Fire State Park** and **Red Rock Canyon National Conservation Area** offer dramatic views of towering rust-colored sandstone formations and abundant opportunities for hiking and picnicking. A few miles from Red Rock Canyon, children will especially enjoy the petting zoo, miniature train rides and staged gunfights at **Bonnie Springs Old Nevada**. Only 45 minutes from Las Vegas is **Spring Mountains National Recreation Area** (part of Humboldt-Toiyabe National Forest), where mountain scenery, cooler temperatures and, in season, snow skiing can be found. **Lake Mead National Recreation Area**, 20 miles east of Las Vegas, has year-round fishing, swimming, hiking and picnicking, as well as guided tours of magnificent **Hoover Dam**.

The Ramada Express has an on-site **narrow-gauge railroad** with a steam locomotive that takes passengers for a ride around the parking lot. The train consists of an engine and two open-air passenger cars, which have a combined capacity of 65 passengers. The rides are free and the train operates daily. Inside the hotel there is also a play area for young children that features a train.

A trip to the old mining town of **Oatman** will prove to be a treat for all ages. A group of friendly but wild burros roam the streets, often greeting visitors in hopes of a snack (carrots are sold at local stores). Entertaining gunfights are staged on most weekends and holidays, and the town is fraught with small antique and souvenir shops that may be of interest to older children.

Children might also enjoy a trip to see **American Indian petroglyphs** in Grapevine Canyon, the local artifacts at the **Colorado River Museum**, the exotic cars at **Don Laughlin's Classic Car Collection** or a close-up look at **Davis Dam**. There are also plenty of opportunities for **hiking**, **fishing** and **swimming**; Davis Camp County Park is an excellent place for all three. (See listings in the *Laughlin-Bullhead City* chapter.)

*Friendly engineers and conductors take passengers around the parking lot on a narrow-gauge train at the Ramada Express Hotel in Laughlin.*

# ▼ *Tipping*

A tip, or gratuity, for services rendered is customary in Las Vegas, as it is in any U.S. city. Although entirely at the customer's discretion, prompt, friendly and good quality service traditionally merits a tip. In Las Vegas and Laughlin, there is an especially staggering array of service personnel—all who supplement their income with tips—including card dealers, slot people, showroom maitre d's and pool attendants. When in doubt about the amount, 15 to 20 percent of the total bill is usually appropriate. Following are some helpful guidelines:

**Bartenders/Cocktail Waitresses**—For parties of two to four people, a tip of $1 per round is standard; more for larger groups.

**Bell Captains, Bellmen, Skycaps**—Luggage is usually tipped at $1-2 per bag or around $5 if you have several bags. If you plan on using the concierge or VIP services for arrangements for shows, travel or car, a $5 tip is appropriate.

**Child Care Attendants**—Baby-sitting is no easy task, so a tip of $2-5 for two to four hours of child-care service is appreciated.

**Dealers**—It is customary make a small bet for the dealer or tip a chip when you are winning.

**Hotel Maids**—A tip upon departure of $1 per day is appreciated.

**Lounge Attendants**—Approximately 50 cents to $1 in the attendant's tray is appropriate for being handed towels, soap, etc.

**Masseuse/Masseur**—The 15- to 20-percent rule is standard.

**Pool Attendants**—Fifty cents to $1 is customary for towels, pads, lounges, etc.

**Showroom Maitre d's**—For unassigned restaurant-style seating, it is customary to tip the maitre d' from $5-10 to improve location—up to $20 or more for the really big acts. No tips are required at shows with assigned seating.

**Slot People/Keno Runners**—A $1 tip now and then is appropriate for good service from keno runners and slot people.

**Taxi Drivers**—A tip of $1-2 for a direct route is expected, more if the driver is friendly and helps with the door and your luggage.

**Tour Guides**—A tip of $1-2 per person at the end of the trip is suggested.

**Valet Parking Attendants**—A tip of $1-2 is standard.

**Waiters/Room Service**—The 15- to 20-percent rule applies for both. With room service, the tip is sometimes included in the bill; be sure to ask when you place your order.

# Shopping

Most of the big resort hotels in Las Vegas and Laughlin have shopping arcades. These usually feature a dozen or so stores selling designer fashions, furs, jewelry, artwork, toys and inter-national gifts. One of the largest of these arcades is in Las Vegas at **Bally's Casino Resort**, which boasts 40 stores. **Sam's Town**, east of the Strip at Flamingo Road and Boulder Highway in Las Vegas, features a huge Western-wear emporium; its 40,000 square feet of retail space makes it one of the largest such stores west of the Rockies. Another large, elaborate mall is **The Forum Shops at Caesars**, which doubled its size in 1997 to more than half a million square feet; it's perhaps best known for its sky-like ceiling with lighting that changes from "day" to "night" in less than an hour. Other notable shopping centers and factory outlets in Las Vegas include the **Boulevard Mall, Chinatown Plaza, Factory Stores of America, Belz Factory Outlet World** and the **Meadows and Fashion Show malls**. (See *Las Vegas Valley* chapter for more detailed listings.)

The larger hotels are also good places to find shops that carry such necessities as aspirin, toothbrushes, film, postage stamps, magazines and other sundries. These shops are usually centrally located near the front entrance of the hotel, the registration desk or the casino. In addition to the numerous shopping outlets in Las Vegas, Laughlin boasts the new **Horizon Outlet Center** at the corner of Casino Drive and Edison Way. The 225,000-square-foot mall features more than 50 food and retail outlets, a movie theater and a basement garage with 1220 parking spaces.

For the real souvenir hound there is also no shortage of trinket shops. Hats, shirts, coffee mugs, salt and pepper shakers, genuine leather purses, Indian dolls, turquoise jewelry, dice, playing cards and poker chips are widely available. In Las Vegas, these shops are mainly along the Strip area of Las Vegas Boulevard from Charleston Boulevard south to Tropicana Avenue. Downtown, they are located one block off Fremont between Main and 4th streets.

*The Forum Shops at Caesars Palace offers upscale shopping in a Roman village setting.*

# History

*Las Vegas is Spanish for "The Meadows," so named for its numerous springs and once verdant landscape. The surrounding harsh and unforgiving Mojave Desert protected this oasis for centuries from all but the native Paiute Indians. It was not until 1829 when the first known non-Indian set foot on the land. By comparison, Laughlin is a much more recent arrival, beginning in 1966 with Don Laughlin's aerial view of the area's barren, formidable landscape. From his private plane, the native Midwesterner saw investment potential along a vacant stretch of the Colorado River, next to the then 11-year-old Davis Dam and the sparsely populated town of Bullhead City, Arizona.*

The discovery of abundant spring water at what is now Las Vegas shortened the Spanish Trail to Los Angeles, eased the rigors for Spanish traders and hastened the rush west for California gold. Some 14 years later, John C. Frémont, an American soldier and explorer, led an overland expedition west and camped at Las Vegas Springs. Fremont Street and numerous other area landmarks carry his name.

The modern history of Las Vegas began in 1855, when a small group of Mormon settlers arrived. They came to protect the mail route between Los Angeles and Salt Lake City, but for the next three years were also engaged in fruit and vegetable cultivation and lead mining at Potosi Mountain.

The Mormons abandoned their mining activity when the bullets made from their ore proved to be flaky and brittle due to an extremely high silver content—a problem other miners would liked to have had. Raids by local Indians also added to their problems. The Mormons' 150-square-foot adobe fort was abandoned in 1858; a portion of it can be seen today near the intersection of Las Vegas Boulevard North and Washington Avenue (see Old Las Vegas Mormon Fort State Historic Park in the *Las Vegas Valley* chapter).

After the Mormons' departure, the area was left to the native tribes. In 1864 Nevada was admitted to the Union as the 36th state, although the 11,000 square miles surrounding Las Vegas were part of the Arizona territory. It was not until two years later that Congress ceded the region to Nevada, establishing the current state borders.

Farming and ranching were the main focus of Las Vegas until the coming of the railroad. On May 15, 1905, the Union Pacific Railroad auctioned off 1200 lots in a single day—lots that soon sprouted gambling houses, saloons and stores. In 1910 Nevada passed an anti-gambling law so strict that it even forbade the western custom of flipping a coin for the price of a drink. Despite the law, which remained in effect for 20 years, gambling continued to flourish in the form of "underground" games, where patrons uttered a secret password to play.

Legalized gambling returned to the state in 1931, at the height of the Great Depression. It was also the same year construction started on the Boulder Canyon Project. Thousands of jobless citizens, victims of the nation's economic slump, streamed into the Las Vegas-Boulder City area for work. At its peak, the project employed 5128 people and had an average monthly

*Fremont Street (1929) as Las Vegas awaits inspection as a housing center for thousands of Boulder Dam (Hoover Dam) construction workers.*

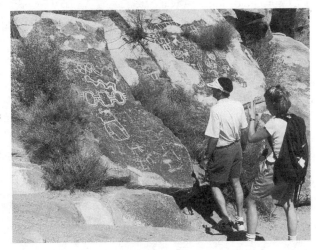

*Petroglyphs in Grapevine Canyon (near Laughlin) show evidence of the region's Indian heritage.*

payroll of $500,000. In 1935 President Franklin Roosevelt dedicated the structure, known then as "Boulder Dam." In April 1947, by congressional action, the 726-foot-high structure was officially designated Hoover Dam, the name by which it is known today.

The great hydroelectric project on the Colorado River originally brought power to Las Vegas, and this abundant source of electricity helped create the famous neon city. (Today Las Vegas' power primarily comes from coal burning power stations.) In 1940 a group of Los Angeles investors, speculating on the resort potential of the area, built El Rancho Vegas, the first hotel on what became the Las Vegas Strip. Shortly thereafter, the Last Frontier was completed, followed by the fabulous Flamingo, a hotel and casino built by the infamous mobster Benjamin "Bugsy" Siegel. (Six months after the

Flamingo's 1946 opening, Siegel was murdered by an unknown assailant in Beverly Hills, California.)

The momentum established by these early resorts has continued ever since, taking off in the post-World War II years as the town emerged to become a major tourist destination. High-rise hotels with blazing marquees began to rise along a stretch of Las Vegas Boulevard that would soon be known as simply the Strip. The Riviera, Stardust, Hacienda and Dunes were but a few of those to open during the 1950s, and their names soon became familiar far beyond the Nevada state line.

Casino gambling was the main draw at most venues, but entertainment helped seal Las Vegas' reputation as a playground getaway. In 1941, when El Rancho Las Vegas was the only Strip resort, singers, comedians, strippers and other performers entertained guests in its small, intimate showroom.

Other resorts copied that successful format by headlining big-name entertain-

ers of their own. The Stardust blazed a new path in the 1950s when it made a stage spectacular its main entertainment feature. The hotel imported Lido de Paris from France, a critically acclaimed show that enjoyed a 31-year run before being replaced by the present-day production, "Enter the Night." The Tropicana followed suit with another French import when it bought the U.S. rights to the "Folies Bergere" in 1960. It remains a favorite to this day.

Casino lounges emerged as well during the post-war years, offering dusk-to-dawn entertainment while spawning stars like Don Rickles, Buddy Hackett, Alan King and the Mary Kaye Trio. Meanwhile, the famed "Rat Pack" of Frank Sinatra, Dean Martin and Sammy Davis Jr. crooned to hundreds of sellout audiences during their hey-days in the 1950s and '60s. Sinatra would remain a star attraction decades later, packing the crowds in till the early 1990s.

No one did more for the town's entertainment image, however, than the King himself, Elvis Presley. By 1964, when he

*Rising like an oasis in the desert is Primm, once a mere border casino and now boasting three hotel-casinos featuring thrill rides and swimming pools, as well as name big-entertainment.*

romanced Ann-Margaret in the film "Viva Las Vegas," he had established himself as a major Strip attraction, and his greatest glory days still lay ahead. Between 1969 and 1976 Presley performed to more than 1500 sellout crowds at the Las Vegas Hilton, a one-man windfall for the town's tourism business.

While gambling remained the number one lure, in 1976 the town faced competition for the first time when New Jersey voters approved a ballot measure to open casinos in Atlantic City. Las Vegas confronted the challenge by transforming itself to a family-friendly destination. As early as 1968, Circus Circus opened on the Strip, with carnival games and midway-style rides beneath its circus tent-shaped roof, but the transformation did not take off until the late 1980s.

When the Mirage opened in 1989, it featured a white tiger habitat, dolphin pool and man-made volcano among its many noncasino attractions. A year later came the Excalibur, a 4000-room property designed like a medieval castle with jousting knights, court jesters and entire floors devoted to nongambling entertainment. The '90s building frenzy was under way, reaching its peak (so far) in late 1993 when three huge properties, the Luxor, Treasure Island and MGM Grand, opened within three months of each other. With 5005 rooms, the MGM Grand became the world's largest hotel property.

Population has grown dramatically at the same time, as Las Vegas swelled from 258,000 residents in 1990 to 405,000 by mid-1997. Likewise, Clark County is now home to more than 1.1 million people, compared to 768,000 when the decade began. By some esti-mates that figure could top 1.5 million by the year 2010.

Perhaps befitting that growth, Las Vegas has never paid great homage to its history, choosing instead to focus on tomorrow. As an example, when Hilton Corporation tore down an older section of the Flamingo Hotel in 1993, it also razed the fortress-like "Bugsy Suite" with its false stairways and bulletproof office that the gangster used before his death. The Flamingo name survives, but each year entire hotels of bygone eras are felled to clear the way for big-ger, more elaborate resorts than ever before.

Even when Las Vegas does preserve the past, it reinvents it to maintain the interest of visitors' ever-changing tastes. Take Fremont Street, the famed "Glitter Gulch," which had lost out years ago to the Strip as the center of gambling and entertainment action. A four-block section of the street was closed to traffic in 1995 and trans-formed into the Fremont Street Experience, a pedestrian mall crowned by a 90-foot-high canopy with more than 2 million lights. The street now hosts a series of dazzling sound and light shows on the hour every night.

Looking ahead, several more mega-hotels are under construction or in the planning stages that will further raise the ante both for size and elaborate-ness. The biggest is the Venetian, a Venice-themed resort that will have 6000 guestrooms when completed. Scheduled to open in 1999, the new property is rising at the site of the for-mer Sands Hotel Casino, imploded by dynamite in 1996.

As the 21st century unfolds, water shortfalls may slow the region's long-term growth. Most of Las Vegas' water comes from the Colorado River, which Nevada must share with seven other states. If present trends continue, the state will use up its allotment within 10 years, curtailing growth if new supplies are not developed.

Before 1966, what is now **Laughlin** was composed of one roadhouse restaurant at the end of a dirt road. The area was known as South Pointe, the name of a construction camp that housed workers for nearby Davis Dam. (South Pointe's population disappeared following completion of the dam in 1953.) Entrepreneur Don Laughlin, fresh from a successful 10-year gaming venture in Las Vegas, purchased and renovated the deteriorating restaurant as a casino in 1966, naming it appropriately "Riverside." In 1977 the growing community was officially named after its entrepreneur-founder.

Initially, Laughlin's customers were residents of Bullhead City, enticed by the free ferry service from a parking lot on the Arizona side of the river. As news of the friendly, informal atmosphere of the Riverside casino got out, people from greater distances showed up. Soon the new business was a great success, which induced Laughlin to expand his operation. Others quickly saw the potential for the gaming business along the shores of the Colorado, so beginning in 1967 with what is now the Golden Nugget (originally called the Bob Cat), additional casino/hotels began to rise. Today nine major casinos occupy the west riverbank of the Colorado at Laughlin; another sits a block back from the water, and still another lies nine miles to the south of town on the Fort Mojave Indian Reservation. Those casinos were the main draw to the 4.6 million people who visited Laughlin in 1996.

Across the river in Bullhead City, the boomtown atmosphere is equally intense. Rugged mountains provide a scenic backdrop and contain mines and ghost towns of historic importance. Katherine Mine, Chloride and Oatman give travelers an enticing glimpse into the world of the Wild West. A drive along historic Route 66 through Oatman and Kingman, Arizona, is not only pleasing to the eye, with the area's wonderfully jagged mountaintops, winding roads and alluring vistas, but it serves as a reminder of those who migrated from the parched midwest during the 1930s on this very road, seeking a better life. More than 28,000 people reside in Bullhead City today.

In 1987, Laughlin supplanted Lake Tahoe as Nevada's third-largest gaming resort (after Las Vegas and Reno), and plans for further growth are a major topic of local conversation. Laughlin has clearly come a long way from its humble beginnings, when coyotes outnumbered the town's population. The town's 8,500 residents are still outnumbered, however, this time by more than 11,000 slot machines.

Then there's **Primm**, the latest town to make a pitch for the hearts and wallets of visitors to Southern Nevada. Known for years as Stateline, the town changed its name in 1996 to honor Gary Primm, who owns the three hotel-casinos in this outpost at the California state line. Once just a dusty rest stop along I-15, Primm has become a destination in its own right with its modern hotel-casinos, thrill rides and the brand-new Primm Valley Golf Club, which opened in mid-1997.

# Casino Games

*From 1931 until the mid-1970s, Nevada was the only state that offered legalized gambling. This fact alone helped make Las Vegas the single most popular tourist destination in the United States. The profits from gambling are enormous, and most efforts to attract new visitors could not be underwritten without the lucrative casinos.*

Before embarking on one or more of the many games of chance, it's a good idea to become familiar with a game's rules and strategy. Gambling instruction is offered in most casinos and, in some cases, on the hotel's cable television channel. Understanding the intricacies of a game will not only increase your odds of winning but also make it more enjoyable to play. Do not expect dealers or croupiers to be of much help; they have a job to do and will offer assistance and advice only when they can. A good way to get to know a game is to watch the action for a while before joining in; observation is a cheap way of learning some of the more obvious lessons.

There are many books devoted to the art of casino gambling. These books have complete explanations of the rules, strategy, odds, wagering and systems that claim to give players an advantage. But be skeptical of the systems: statistically they might work in the long run, but few players have the time and the resources to last, or the concentration and mental dexterity that are often required. The serious student will spend some time practicing at home before venturing into a casino to test his or her mettle. And finally, a last piece of advice: Before placing any bets, determine how much you can afford to lose and set that money aside for gambling. Should it cross to the other side of the tables, don't dig for more! It is not just a cliché that people can lose everything they have.

**BACCARAT** A game very similar to chemin de fer, baccarat (pronounced Ba-Ca-Rah) is played with eight decks of cards dealt from a box called a "shoe." Two cards are given to each of two players, with one player being designated the bank. The object of the game is to come as close to the number nine as possible. All tens and face cards are counted as zero. Other people at the table bet on either the bank or the player.

**BINGO** Most bingo games in Las Vegas and Laughlin are played on "boards" with three bingo cards on each board. There are both open-play and party bingo at most casinos. In open-play bingo, each board costs between 10¢ and 40¢ per game. Party bingo is played at set hours; cards cost $1 to $4 each with a $3 to $6 minimum; approximately 10 to 12 games are played during each party session.

**BLACKJACK** Also called "21," blackjack is one of the most popular card games, mainly because it's fast and easy to learn. The object of the game is to beat the dealer by getting as close to 21 as possible without going over that count.

**CRAPS** By far the most complicated casino game, craps offers literally dozens of different ways to bet on the dice. The action is fast and the amount of money exchanging hands is considerable. Craps is not a good game for the timid, but it's great fun to watch.

**KENO** This is an adaptation of an ancient Chinese game. Players mark a series of favorite numbers between one and 80 that appear on the blank keno ticket. Twenty numbers are then drawn at random. The amount of money won depends on the type of ticket played and how many winning numbers were selected. Many restaurants and lounges have keno runners who take the bets. Keno is also a popular game to play on slot machines.

**PAI GOW** This ancient Chinese game involves 32 dominoes that are shuffled by the dealer and then placed in eight stacks of four each. Up to eight players are dealt one stack. The object of the game is to set the four dominoes into two pairs for the best ranking combinations.

**PAI GOW POKER** This game is a combination of poker and Pai Gow. It is played with an ordinary deck of 52 cards plus one joker. The joker is used as an ace or to complete a straight or flush. Players are dealt seven cards each, which are arranged into two hands. One hand contains five cards and is known as the "high hand," while the other hand has only two cards and is called the "low hand." The object of the game is to win the bet by having both the high and low hands rank higher than the respective hands of the banker. The ranking is determined by traditional poker rules.

**POKER** The rules are pretty much the same for casino poker as they are for home games, except that the house provides a dealer who manages the game without playing a hand. The house makes money by taking a small percentage of each pot. Check the rules carefully before sitting down at a game.

**RACE AND SPORTS BOOKS** Bets can be made on practically any horse race, boxing match, or professional or collegiate game (as long as it does not involve a Nevada event) from the comfort of race and sports books. Live events are shown on giant, satellite-fed screens. Most of the major hotels have race and sports books.

**ROULETTE** The roulette wheel has 36 numbers plus a green zero and a green double zero. Bets can be made on one number, a group, a color or a column of numbers. Odds on roulette range from 35-to-1 to even money. For example, if the player wins by betting on a single number, he or she is paid $35 for every $1 wagered. This is strictly a game of luck and intuition, so there's no reason to worry about skill level. Low stakes games are common, so a few dollars can keep a player going for quite some time.

**SLOT MACHINES** One-armed-bandits and video poker comprise the majority of slots, but gamblers will also find video blackjack, video keno and a variety of other casino games offered. Nickel, quarter and dollar machines are the most prevalent, and today most slots don't even require coins or tokens—they accept U.S. bills of many denominations. There are a variety of ways to win, including multiple pay lines, fixed jackpots and progressives (slots linked to statewide networks). To win the big jackpots and progressives requires more than the minimum bet; some machines accept up to 10 bets (or coins) at once.

# Marriage Information

*In Las Vegas, two words spoken as frequently as "hit me" and "double down" are with-out a doubt, "I do." Where else but in this unique desert community are marriage licenses issued so swiftly (one every 5½ minutes) and Elvis impersonators preside over the ceremonies. Seven days a week, 24 hours a day on weekends (correct change required), wedding vows are taken at drive-up windows, on bungee jumping platforms, not to mention from helicopters, on boats and in hotel suites, churches and dozens of wedding chapels. Ninety miles to the south, Laughlin now has its own branch of the Clark County Clerk's Office, and couples there can get hitched on the Colorado River aboard Mississippi-style riverboats or in any number of wedding chapels.*

Marriages in **Las Vegas** total more than 100,000 per year, due in part to the ease of getting a marriage license. Historically, the most popular wedding day here is February 14 (Valentine's Day), with December 31 (New Year's Eve) running a close second. Among the famous who have married in Las Vegas are Elvis and Priscilla Presley, Frank Sinatra and Mia Farrow, Richard Gere and Cindy Crawford, Paul Newman and Joanne Woodward, and Bruce Willis and Demi Moore.

To purchase a marriage license, the bride and groom must simply appear at the Marriage Bureau Office, located in the courthouse at 200 South 3rd Street. No legal residency is required. Blood tests are not needed and there is no waiting period. Persons ages 16 or 17 years of age must have the consent of their parents or legal guardians.

*The "Marriage Capital of the World" weds 100,000 couples each year.*

Proof of age may be required. If the bride or groom was previously married, divorce must be final in the state in which it was granted; no papers are required. The office is open daily; Monday through Thursday from 8 a.m. to midnight, and continuously (24 hours) from 8 a.m. Friday to midnight Sunday; 24 hours on holidays. The license fee is $35. For information, call the Marriage Bureau Office at (702) 455-4415.

Marriage ceremonies can be performed by the Commissioner of Civil Marriages, 309 South 3rd Street, or in one of the many wedding chapels in town (more than 50 at last count). The commissioner's office charges $35, and the hours are the same as the county clerk's office. Wedding chapel fees depend on the elaborateness of the ceremony. Many of the large hotel/casino complexes have wedding chapels on the grounds. For a list of wedding chapels, see the Las Vegas telephone directory yellow pages under "Wedding."

An additional branch of the Clark County Clerk's Office serves the community of **Laughlin**. Couples wishing to marry in this river city can obtain a license at the Justice Court Office in the Regional Government Center, 101 Civic Way. Licenses are issued Monday through Thursday from 8 a.m. to 5 p.m., Friday from 8 a.m. to 8 p.m. and Saturday from 9 a.m. to 5 p.m. No waiting period or blood test is required. All that is necessary is the $35 license fee in cash and proof of age. The Laughlin-Bullhead City area offers wedding services at several wedding chapels and aboard riverboats. Ceremonies can also be performed in the Justice Court Office (appointments are required). There is an additional $35 recording fee here for a total charge of $70. For more information, call the Justice Court Office at (702) 298-4622. Wedding chapels can be found in the Laughlin-Bullhead City telephone directory yellow pages under "Wedding Chapels and Ceremonies."

# Las Vegas Valley

*Today's gambling meccas offer an array of activities for the whole family. Contrary to the adults-only atmosphere of the past, **Las Vegas** now promotes a child-friendly environment that's hard to resist. Roller coasters, water parks, virtual reality theaters, laser shows, and an assortment of museums have sprung up across the city and neighboring communities that comprise the Las Vegas Valley.*

*The biggest change, though, has been the 1990s proliferation of huge, whimsically designed hotels. It's no longer enough to boast how many guest rooms you have or how "loose" the casino slots may be; today's properties have adopted elaborate themes throughout to lure visitors their way. Just drive up from the south end of the Strip, where traffic slows to a crawl while drivers shamelessly gawk at the huge pyramid and full-size sphinx of the Egyptian-themed Luxor. Next door stands the surreal white castle of the Excalibur, which salutes the legend of King Arthur. Just beyond that soars the third-scale Manhattan skyline of New York New York, paying homage to its namesake city. Farther up, snarling pirates and gallant sailors wage battle nightly in front of Treasure Island.*

*The trend shows no signs of playing out, with many more theme resorts under construction or on the drawing boards. Without a doubt, audacious creativity, unabashed flamboyance and a dash of irreverence have proved a winning formula in wooing more and more visitors to modern-day Las Vegas.*

## POINTS OF INTEREST

Attractions are listed alphabetically by city or area—**Henderson**, **Las Vegas** and **North Las Vegas**. Listings connected to hotel properties do not imply AAA endorsement for the lodging establishment.

## Henderson

See A Quick Guide to Las Vegas in this chapter under Las Vegas.

**CLARK COUNTY HERITAGE MUSEUM** *13 miles southeast of Las Vegas at 1830 S. Boulder Hwy. (US 93/95), 89015. (702) 455-7955. Open daily 9 a.m.- 4:30 p.m. Closed Jan. 1 and Dec. 25. Adults, $1.50; ages 55 and over and 3-15, $1.* This 25-acre museum houses regional memorabilia, historic structures and artifacts. Heritage Street's collection of six historic homes and commercial buildings includes many which have been fully restored to reflect the lifestyles of their respective eras. Other outdoor exhibits include authentic rolling stock, mining equipment and a "ghost town" comprised of several structures dating to the 1880s. The 8000-square-foot indoor Exhibit Center features special theme displays, and a permanent Southern Nevada timeline exhibit that dates from prehistoric times to the present.

**CRANBERRY WORLD WEST** *Off Gibson Rd. at 1301 American Pacific Dr., 89014. (702) 566-7160, (800) 289-0917. Open daily 9 a.m.-5 p.m.; call for holiday hours. Free.* The Ocean Spray Visitor Center is the site of this self-guided tour, adjacent to the Henderson processing plant. The tour begins with a six-minute film explaining the history and processing of the cranberry, then offers a glimpse into the bottling operations and a series of interactive exhibits geared to children. At the end of the tour, the demonstration kitchen provides free samples of juice drinks and a variety of cranberry-inspired treats. The gift shop offers a number of gourmet and novelty items for sale.

*Authentic rolling stock and a "ghost town" comprise some of the exhibits at the Clark County Heritage Museum.*

**ETHEL M CHOCOLATES FACTORY** *8 miles southeast of the Strip, off Sunset Wy.; 2 Cactus Garden Dr., 89014. Recorded information (702) 433-2500. Open daily 8:30 a.m.-7 p.m. Closed Thanksgiving and Dec. 25. Free.* Ethel M's self-guided tour offers a behind-the-scenes look at the ingredients and machinery used in the candy-making process. Adjacent to the factory is a 2½-acre cactus garden. At the end of the tour, participants get a chance to sample their favorite Ethel M chocolate and shop for more tempting treats in the gift store.

---

### ▼ *Show Your Card and Save*

Certain attractions offer AAA members a special discount. The discount is given to both adults and children and applies to the member and his or her family traveling together, usually up to six persons. The discount may not apply if any other gate reduction is offered or if tickets are purchased through an agent rather than at the attraction's ticket office. Because attractions offering such discounts change frequently, they are not listed here. For current information on such attractions and discounts, check the most recent edition of the AAA *California/Nevada TourBook*. When in doubt, ask if the discount is available at the time of your visit.

---

**FAVORITE BRANDS MARSHMALLOW FACTORY** *Off Gibson and Mary Crest rds.; 1180 Marshmallow Ln., 89014. (702) 564-3878. Open daily 9 a.m.-4:30 p.m. Closed Sun. and major holidays. Free.* This self-guided tour offers visitors a chance to view the entire marshmallow-making process from start to finish. A free bag of marshmallows is given to each visitor at the end of the tour. Educational games, T-shirts and marshmallow treats can be purchased in the gift shop.

**RON LEE'S WORLD OF CLOWNS** *Off Gibson and Warm Springs rds.; 330 Carousel Pkwy., 89014. (702) 434-3920. Open Mon.-Sat. 9 a.m.-5 p.m. Closed Sun. and major holidays. Free tour; carousel rides, $1.* The mold-making and painting processes of clown and animation figurines are shown during this self-guided tour. Through windows, visitors see the artisans at work;

videos at each station explain the process being done. A large gift shop features the final products for sale, and a gourmet cafe offers sandwiches, salads, pastries, coffee and more. The facility also houses a 30-foot Chance Carousel—a favorite with children.

# Las Vegas

**A.J. HACKETT BUNGEE** *Adjacent to Circus Circus Hotel-Casino; 810 Circus Circus Dr., 89109. (702) 385-4321. Open daily; May through Sep., 10 a.m.-midnight; Oct. through Apr., Mon.-Fri. noon-10 p.m., Sat.-Sun. noon-midnight. Closed Thanksgiving and Dec. 25. $81 per person, additional jumps same day, $20 per person.* This New Zealand-based company has several locations around the world and a record of more than 950,000 incident-free jumps. Participants plunge 175 feet from North America's highest double platform over a 13-foot pool. Fee includes video and T-shirt.

**BELZ FACTORY OUTLET WORLD** *Corner of Las Vegas Blvd. S. and Warm Springs Rd.; 7400 Las Vegas Blvd. S., 89123. (702) 896-5599. Open daily; Mon.-Sat. 10 a.m.-9 p.m., Sun. to 6 p.m. Smoke-free building.* This 600,000-square-foot indoor mall has 145 outlets and a carousel.

**BOULEVARD MALL** *Maryland Pkwy. and Desert Inn Rd.; 3528 S. Maryland Pkwy., 89109. (702) 732-8949. Open daily; Mon.-Fri. 10 a.m.-9 p.m., Sat. 10 a.m.-8 p.m., Sun. 11 a.m.-6 p.m. Closed Easter, Thanksgiving and Dec. 25.* This 1 million-square-foot indoor mall is the largest shopping center in Nevada.

**BUCCANEER BAY** *Treasure Island, 3300 Las Vegas Blvd. S., 89109. (702) 894-7111. Shows daily at 4, 5:30, 7, 8:30, 10 and 11:30 p.m.; no performances during inclement weather or high winds. Arrive early for best viewing; standing room only. Free.* Located at the

*Chocoholics will crave a visit to the Ethel M Chocolates Factory.*

hotel's main entrance on the Strip, Buccaneer Bay treats passersby to a highly entertaining sea battle between an 80-foot-long pirate ship and a British frigate. The show features live actors, numerous fiery explosions and lots of witty, swashbuckling dialogue.

### CAESARS MAGICAL EMPIRE
*Caesars Palace, 3570 Las Vegas Blvd. S., 89109. (702) 731-7110. Dinner shows daily 4:30-11 p.m. $75-200; discount for early and late seatings. Tours daily 11 a.m.-4 p.m. Free.* Magic, mystery and dining converge in this new attraction, where visitors are entertained before and during their meals. Greeters dressed as Roman sentries lead guests to one of 10 dining chambers or two séance rooms, where a magician takes charge and performs an array of mystical feats during dinner. Tours of the dining/entertainment complex, including a "Lumineria" show with dancing, fire, smoke and lighting effects, are available during pre-dining hours.

### CASHMAN FIELD CENTER
*North of downtown; 850 Las Vegas Blvd. N., 89101. (702) 386-7100.* The center contains two large exhibition halls, a 1954-seat theater and a 10,000-seat baseball field. The Las Vegas Stars professional baseball club of the Pacific Coast League plays at this location from early April through September.

### CHINATOWN PLAZA *West of the Strip; 4255 Spring Mountain Rd., 89102. (702) 221-8448, 222-0590. Open daily; store hours vary.* This shopping plaza has more than two dozen specialty shops that carry jewelry, handcrafted furniture, clothing and other merchandise from the Orient. In addition to several restaurants, one of the largest Oriental supermarkets in Nevada is located here.

### DEBBIE REYNOLDS HOLLYWOOD MOVIE MUSEUM *Debbie Reynolds Hollywood Hotel/Casino, 305 Convention Center Dr., 89109. (702) 734-0711, 733-2243. Open daily; call for hours. Admission is $7.95 per person.* Clips from classic Hollywood films and the elaborate costumes that appeared in them are presented in a specially designed, 80-seat theater with revolving stages. Following the 45-minute show, visitors tour an adjacent museum housing vintage Hollywood props and costumes, including Vivien Leigh's hats from "Gone with the Wind," Marilyn Monroe's famous white dress from "The Seven Year Itch" and Judy Garland's ruby slippers from "The Wizard of Oz."

### DOLPHIN AND SECRET GARDEN HABITATS *The Mirage, 3400 Las Vegas Blvd. S., 89109. (702) 791-7111. Dolphin Habitat open daily; Mon.-Fri. 11 a.m.-5:30 p.m., Sat., Sun. and holidays 10 a.m.-5:30 p.m. Adults, $10, on Wed. $5; ages 9 and under accompanied by an adult, free. White Tiger Habitat open 24 hours; free.* A close look at seven Atlantic Bottlenose Dolphins is the main draw of the Dolphin Habitat, which offers continuous 15-minute tours focused primarily on the facility's underwater viewing room. The Secret Garden features seven zoological environments with animals from the Siegfried & Roy stage show. Another habitat featuring the famous Royal White Tigers of the Siegfried & Roy stage show is located on the hotel's southwestern side, just off the casino. Located behind a floor-to-ceiling wall of glass, these beautiful animals can be observed while they sleep, eat and play.

# ▼ *A Quick Guide to Las Vegas and Vicinity*

## Population
405,254 (City of Las Vegas)
1,136,782 (Clark County)

## Elevation        2174 ft.

## Emergency      911

## Police (nonemergency)
Boulder City        (702) 293-9224
Henderson          (702) 565-8933
Metropolitan Las Vegas, Mount
Charleston and North Las Vegas
                          (702) 649-9111

## Highway Conditions
                          (702) 486-3116

## Time               (702) 844-1212

## Weather
Las Vegas           (702) 248-4800
Mount Charleston,
Lake Mead         (702) 736-3854

## Emergency Road Service for AAA Members
(800) AAA-HELP (in the USA and Canada)
(800) 955-4TDD (for the hearing impaired)

## Newspapers
The major daily newspapers are the *Las Vegas Review Journal* and the *Las Vegas Sun.* The biweekly publication *What's On In Las Vegas,* distributed in hotels, motels and other tourist venues, provides information on local attractions, dining and entertainment.

## Radio Stations
**Christian:** KILA (90.5 FM), KKVV (1060 AM); **Classic Rock:** KKLZ (96.3 FM), KOMP (92.3 FM),
KXTE (107.5 FM); **Contemporary/Rock:** KCEP (88.1 FM), KLUC (98.5 FM), KMZQ (100.5 FM), KSNE (106.5 FM), KXPT (97.1 FM), KMXB (94.1 FM); **Country:** KFMS (102 FM), KIXW (101.5/107.3 FM), KWNR (95.5 FM); **Highway News:** KHWY (98.5 FM); **Jazz:** KUNV (91.5 FM); **News/Sports/Talk:** KDWN (720 AM), KENO (1460 AM), KLAV (1230 AM), KORK (920 AM), KVBC (105.1 FM), KNXT (840 AM), KNEWS (970 AM); **Oldies:** KBGO (93.1 FM), KOOL (105.5 FM); **Public Radio/Classical:** KNPR (89.5 FM); **Spanish:** KDOL (1280 AM). For a complete list of radio programs, consult the daily newspapers.

## TV Stations
The area's major television stations include channels 3 (NBC), 5 (FOX), 8 (CBS), 10 (PBS), 13 (ABC), 21 (UPN), 33 (WB) and 39 (Spanish). For a complete list of television programs, consult the daily newspapers.

## Public Transportation
The **Downtown Transportation Center**, located at Stewart Avenue and Casino Center Boulevard, serves as a transportation hub for Citizens Area Transit (CAT) buses and the downtown trolley. Most bus lines connect to the center, as does the trolley system. The center is open daily; Monday-Friday 6 a.m.-10 p.m.; Saturday, Sunday and holidays 6 a.m.-6 p.m. In addition to ticket and route information personnel, the facility also has a restaurant.

**Bus** *(702) 228-7433 (CAT-RIDE). One-way fares for routes 301 and 303:*

adults, $1.50; ages 62 and over, 5-17 and persons with disabilities, 50¢. One-way fares for all other routes: adults, $1; ages 62 and over, 5-17 and persons with disabilities, 50¢. **Exact change is required.** Tokens (called CAT Coins) or a monthly pass can be purchased at the Downtown Transportation Center. One easy way to travel from place to place on the Strip, or between the Strip and downtown, is to take the CAT bus. Daily from 5 a.m. to midnight, the CAT bus (Route 301) runs at 10-minute intervals north and south along the Strip between the southernmost point, Vacation Village, and the northernmost point, the Downtown Transportation Center. From midnight to 5 a.m., the bus takes the same route but at 15-minute intervals. The Strip Express (Route 302) runs this same route daily at 15-minute intervals from 6 p.m. to midnight.

The CAT bus (Route 303) provides hourly service from 5:30 a.m. to 12:30 a.m. from Vacation Village south to Belz Factory Outlet World and Factory Stores of America. Northbound service runs hourly from 6 a.m. to 1 a.m.

Local residential bus service to several areas, including Henderson and Boulder City, is also available. Call for more information.

**Downtown Trolley** *(702) 229-6024. Fares: adults, 50¢; ages 62 and over, ages 17 and under, 25¢; disabled ride free.* Shuttle buses designed to look like trolleys depart the Downtown Transportation Center daily every 20 minutes from 7:30 a.m. to 11 p.m. The route traveled is along Ogden Avenue (eastbound) to the Charleston Plaza Shopping Center and Fremont Street (westbound). The entire route takes 30 minutes to travel. (Do not confuse this trolley with the Strip trolley—the routes connect at the Stratosphere Tower, but riders must pay for both of them.) See the *Downtown Las Vegas* map.

Trolley service to Meadows Mall is also provided 10 times a day, Monday through Saturday 10:30 a.m. to 5 p.m. There is no Sunday or holiday service. Fares: adults, $1.10; ages 62 and over, persons with disabilities, and ages 17 and under, 55¢.

**Strip Trolley** *(702) 382-1404. Fare: $1.30.* Like the downtown trolley, the Strip trolley also uses shuttle buses designed to look like trolleys. The trolleys operate daily 9:30 a.m. to 2 a.m. along Las Vegas Boulevard South from the Luxor Las Vegas on the south end to the Stratosphere Tower on the north end. An additional loop includes the Las Vegas Hilton and a portion of Paradise Road. The trolleys pass by each stop about every 15 minutes. (Do not confuse this trolley with the downtown trolley—the routes connect at the Stratosphere Tower but riders must pay for both of them.) See the *Las Vegas Strip* map.

**Taxi** *$2.20 base fare plus $1.50 per mile; 30¢ per minute for standing still. Pickups at McCarran International Airport: $1.20 tax per load.* For visitors who come to Las Vegas to enjoy gaming and entertainment, a trouble-free and economical way of getting around is by cab. Taxis are plentiful, particularly at the entrances of the major resort hotels, and using them helps avoid the nuisance of having to find a parking space in a crowded lot. In addition, if two or three people share one taxi, it compares favorably to the cost of the bus, and there is usually no waiting. A typical trip half the length of the Strip will cost between $10 and $17; from the airport to the middle of the Strip, $10 to $12; and from the airport to downtown, $16 to $24.

Visitors who are staying at a hotel or motel not frequented by cabs or who wish to arrange for a taxi at a particular time may phone any of the following companies for service in Las Vegas. Upon request, ABC Union, Ace, NLV and Western provide vans with wheelchair lifts at regular taxi rates.

| | |
|---|---|
| ABC Union | (702) 736-8444 |
| Ace | (702) 736-8383 |
| Checker/Star/Yellow | |
| | (702) 873-2227 |
| Desert | (702) 386-9102 |
| Henderson | (702) 384-2322 |
| Nellis | (702) 252-0201 |
| NLV | (702) 643-1041 |
| Western | (702) 382-7100 |
| Whittlesea Blue | (702) 384-6111 |

## Hospitals
Desert Springs Hospital
2075 E. Flamingo Rd.
Las Vegas 89119
(702) 733-8800

Lake Mead Hospital Medical Center
1409 E. Lake Mead Blvd.
North Las Vegas 89030
(702) 649-7711

St. Rose Dominican Hospital
102 E. Lake Mead Dr.
Henderson 89015
(702) 564-2622

Sunrise Hospital and Medical Center
3186 S. Maryland Pkwy.
Las Vegas 89109
(702) 731-8000

University Medical Center
1800 W. Charleston Blvd.
Las Vegas 89102
(702) 383-2000

Valley Hospital Medical Center
620 Shadow Ln.
Las Vegas 89106
(702) 388-4000

## AAA/California State Automobile Association
Henderson District Office
601 Whitney Ranch Dr., #A
Henderson 89014
(702) 458-2323
Office hours: Mon.-Fri. 8:30 a.m.-5 p.m.

Las Vegas District Office
3312 W. Charleston Blvd.
Las Vegas 89102
(702) 870-9171
Office hours: Mon.-Fri. 8:30 a.m.-5 p.m.

## Visitor Services
Boulder City Chamber of Commerce
1305 Arizona St.
Boulder City 89005
(702) 293-2034
Office hours: Mon.-Fri. 9 a.m.-5 p.m.

Las Vegas Convention and Visitors Authority
3150 Paradise Rd.
Las Vegas 89109
(702) 892-7575, 892-0711
Office hours: Mon.-Fri. 8 a.m.-6 p.m., Sat.-Sun. 8 a.m.-5 p.m.

Nevada Welcome Center
100 Nevada Hwy.
Boulder City 89005
No phone
Office hours: Daily 8:30 a.m.- 4:30 p.m.

## EXCALIBUR HOTEL & CASINO
*3850 Las Vegas Blvd. S., 89109 (702) 597-7777; (800) 937-7777. Dragon battle staged nightly on the hour, dusk-midnight; motion theater open daily 10 a.m.-11:30 p.m., $3 per person.* This huge, castle-shaped hotel is themed throughout after the medieval days of King Arthur. Among the attractions are two motion simulator theaters, medieval-themed midway games, strolling entertainers and the Court Jester's Stage, where performances take place throughout the day. Outside at the hotel's moat-style entrance, a fire-breathing dragon battles Merlin the magician nightly.

## FACTORY STORES OF AMERICA
*9155 Las Vegas Blvd. S., 89123. (702) 897-9090. Open daily; Mon.-Sat. 10 a.m.-8 p.m., Sun. to 6 p.m.* More than 50 factory outlet stores are featured at this open-air shopping center, including a sports bar with slot machines.

## FASHION SHOW MALL
*Next to Treasure Island, at corner of Las Vegas Blvd. S. and Spring Mountain Rd.; 3200 Las Vegas Blvd. S., 89109. (702) 369-8382. Open daily; Mon.-Fri. 10 a.m.-9 p.m., Sat. to 7 p.m., Sun. noon-6 p.m.* The enclosed, two-level mall houses five department stores and over 140 specialty shops and eateries, including the popular Dive! restaurant. Lighted underground parking accommodates more than 1500 cars.

## THE FORUM SHOPS AT CAESARS
*Caesars Palace, 3500 Las Vegas Blvd. S., 89109. (702) 893-4800. Open Sun.-Thu. 10 a.m-11 p.m., Fri.-Sat. to midnight.* This upscale indoor mall features a Roman motif, talking statues and a domed "sky" that changes colors. A 1997 expansion doubled the mall's size to 533,000 square feet, with a total of more than 110 shops and restaurants. The centerpiece of the new construction is a hall 160 feet in diameter with an 85-foot-high ceiling, featuring a display called "Atlantis" with animated figures.

## FREMONT STREET EXPERIENCE
*Fremont St. from 4th to Main sts. in downtown Las Vegas. (702) 678-5600. Free nightly shows on the hour. Free acrobatic performances Mon.-Sat. at 4:30, 5:30, 6:30 and 7:30 p.m.* The four blocks of downtown known as "Glitter Gulch" have been transformed into a pedestrian-only zone covered by a 90-foot-high latticed canopy embedded with 2.1 million lights. Dubbed the

*Dive! restaurant is a prominent feature at the Fashion Show Mall.*

*The Imperial Palace Auto Collection features changing exhibits of classic, antique and special-interest autos, trucks and motorcycles.*

Fremont Street Experience, this $70 million attraction features high-tech, computer-controlled light and music. In addition, the Doveiko Aerialists, stars of the Moscow Circus, perform their acrobatic show in elaborate Russian costumes with traditional folk music.

**GAMEWORKS** *In Showcase Mall, 3785 Las Vegas Blvd. S.; 89108. (702) 432-4263. Open daily 10 a.m.-2 a.m., Fri.-Sat. to 4 a.m. Game prices vary.* This two-level virtual-reality arcade, created by Steven Spielberg, Sega Enterprises and Universal Studios, touts almost 300 video games of every description. Players can try their luck on ski slopes, battlefields and raceways, among the many attractions. The centerpiece is "Surge Rock," a 75-foot-tall rock-climbing structure.

**GRAND SLAM CANYON ADVEN-TUREDOME** *Adjacent to the Circus Circus Hotel at 2880 Las Vegas Blvd. S.,* *89109. Recorded information (702) 794-3939. Hours vary; call. $15.95 for 48" and taller; $11.95 for 33"-48"; individual ride ticket prices vary. Military and Nev. residents, $2 off adult unlimited ride pass.* Beneath Grand Slam Canyon's shiny pink dome is a climate-controlled amusement park spanning five acres. Featured rides include the nation's only double-loop, double-corkscrew indoor roller coaster; a water flume ride with a 60-foot free fall; Hot Shots Laser Tag, a high-tech version of the old game of tag; and a number of tamer attractions suitable for younger children. Themed gift shops, a restaurant and snack bar are also on premises.

**GUINNESS WORLD OF RECORDS MUSEUM AND GIFT SHOP** *2780 Las Vegas Blvd. S., 89109. (702) 792-3766. Open daily at 9 a.m.; Labor Day to Memorial Day to 6 p.m., rest of year to 8 p.m. Adults, $4.95; ages 62 and over, students and military, $3.95; ages 5-11, $2.95.* Rare videos and artifacts commemorate the world's fastest, greatest, rarest and richest feats from the worlds of entertainment, art, sports and science. Literally thousands of records can be accessed from the "Guinness World of Records" and "World of Sports" data banks. Displays offer visitors the chance to match their height with the world's tallest man and shortest woman, and their weight with that of the world's heaviest man. The "world" of Las Vegas is featured in a display highlighting the city's history, its casinos and entertainers.

## HOLY COW CASINO, CAFE AND BREWERY
*2423 Las Vegas Blvd. S., 89104. (702) 732-2697. Open 24 hours. Free tours 4 times daily; call for schedule. Parking lot adjacent.* Opened in 1993 as Las Vegas' original microbrewery, Holy Cow uses traditional brewing methods and features several award-winning brews. Cow enthusiasts will appreciate the cow accents throughout the interior and the "cowlectibles" sold in the gift shop. The restaurant serves a variety of American-style fare.

## IMPERIAL PALACE AUTO COLLECTION
*Imperial Palace Hotel, 3535 Las Vegas Blvd. S., 89109. (702) 794-3174. Open daily 9:30 a.m.-11:30 p.m. Adults, $6.95; ages 65 and over and 12 and under, $3.* This auto museum, located on the fifth level of the hotel's parking structure, features more than 200 antique, classic and special-interest autos, antique trucks, motorcycles and cars once owned by gangsters and world-famous celebrities. It also houses the world's largest collection of Model J Duesenbergs. The collection contains more than 800 vehicles, which are rotated on a bimonthly basis.

## LAS VEGAS CONVENTION CENTER
*3150 Paradise Rd., 89109.*

*(702) 892-0711.* With 1.3 million square feet of meeting and exhibit space, the convention center is one of the largest single-level facilities in the world. A rotunda, four large meeting halls, numerous meeting rooms and an on-site restaurant allow the facility to host a range of activities, from small groups to conventions of more than 100,000 people. At publication deadline the center was in the midst of a $45-million expansion, due for completion in mid-1998, increasing its total area to 1.9 million square feet.

## LAS VEGAS MINI GRAND PRIX
*1401 N. Rainbow Blvd., 89108. (702) 259-7000. Open daily 10 a.m.-10 p.m.; closed Dec. 25. Call for prices.* This motor amusement center features race tracks where children and adults alike can test their driving skills. Vehicles range from "Kiddie Karts" and go-karts to grand prix cars and "super stock cars." Snack bar on site.

## LAS VEGAS MOTOR SPEEDWAY
*7000 Las Vegas Blvd. N., 89115. (702) 644-4444. Call for ticket prices and program information.* This racing complex hosts a wide range of events throughout the year, most prominently the Las Vegas 400 NASCAR race each March on the 1.5-mile oval. Several smaller tracks accommodate everything from drag racing to road course racing events.

### University of Motor Sports
*Various locations inside speedway. (702) 644-6433. Call for hours and price information.* Would-be race drivers can choose from among 15 different schools to learn racing techniques in a wide variety of vehicles. Options range from go-karts and BMX bicycles all the way up to dragsters and Winston Cup stock cars.

*The Las Vegas Museum of Natural History has one of the most complete exhibits of animated dinosaur replicas in the Southwest.*

**LAS VEGAS NATURAL HISTORY MUSEUM** *900 Las Vegas Blvd. N., 89101. (702) 384-3466. Open daily 9 a.m.-4 p.m. Adults, $5; ages 55 and over, students and military, $4; ages 4-12, $2.50; ages 3 and under, free.* The museum features an animated dinosaurs exhibit, including a 35-foot tyrannosaurus rex; an international wildlife room with mounted animals including a giraffe; a 3000-gallon tank filled with live sharks; a display of plants and wildlife native to Southern Nevada and the Southwest desert; and a children's room that features hands-on exhibits. There is also a gift shop on premises.

**THE LIBERACE MUSEUM** *2 miles east of the Strip at 1775 E. Tropicana Ave., 89119. (702) 798-5595. Open daily; Mon.-Sat. 10 a.m.-5 p.m., Sun. 1-5 p.m. Adults, $6.95; ages 61 and over, $4.50; students, $3.50; and ages 6-12, $2. Children must be accompanied by an adult.* The museum's collection of memorabilia, antiques and classic cars includes Liberace's million-dollar wardrobe and extensive fur collection, his gold and diamond stage jewelry (including a diamond and platinum candelabra ring), and a Baldwin grand piano inlaid with thousands of etched mirror tiles. Of particular interest are a Czar Nicolas uniform with 22-karat gold braiding, a piano that Chopin once played, and a crucifix presented to Liberace by Pope Pius XII. The museum also houses a library displaying his miniature piano collection, a photographic history of his life and a re-creation of his former office and bedroom. Proceeds from the museum go to the nonprofit Liberace Foundation for the Performing and Creative Arts.

**LIED DISCOVERY CHILDREN'S MUSEUM** *833 Las Vegas Blvd. N., 89101. (702) 382-3445. Open Tue.-Sat. 10 a.m.-5 p.m., Sun. noon-5 p.m. Closed Mon. Adults, $5; military, ages 55 and over and 12-17, $4; ages 3-11, $3; ages 2*

*Lied Discovery Children's Museum features a number of intriguing exhibits for the younger set.*

*Eighteen rare and antique pianos are on display in the Piano Gallery at the Liberace Museum.*

*and under, free.* More than 100 hands-on exhibits are featured in this large museum. Play areas include "Places and Spaces," "What Can I Be?" and "Everyday Living," as well as the Toddler Tower, the Bubble Pavilion and a story phone.

**LUXOR ENTERTAINMENT COMPLEX** *At the Luxor, 3900 Las Vegas Blvd. S., 89119. Recorded information (702) 262-4555. Shows screen daily at 10 a.m., about every 30 minutes. Show admissions $4-5 per person.* The hotel's three levels of Egyptian-themed attractions include a series of three participatory films that use motion simulators and large-screen film projections. "Luxor Live" is a simulated TV talk show done in virtual reality. "Crescendo" and "In Search of the Obelisk" are motion simulator rides. The Imax theater offers two- and three-dimensional movies. There is also the Sega VirtuaLand arcade.

**MAGIC & MOVIE HALL OF FAME** *3555 Las Vegas Blvd. S., 89109. (702) 737-1343, (702) 737-5363. Open Tue.-Sat. 10 a.m.-6 p.m.; call for comedy-magic show times. $9.95 per person; $3 for ages 12 and under.* This museum features a multimillion dollar exhibit of magic, movie and ventriloquist memorabilia. Half-hour-long comedy-magic shows are included with the price of admission.

**MEADOWS MALL** *US 95 at Valley View; 4300 Meadows Ln., 89107. (702) 878-3331. Open daily; Mon.-Fri. 10 a.m.-9 p.m., Sat. and Sun. to 6 p.m.; extended hours during Dec. holiday season. Carousel ride 50¢.* This enclosed mall features a 1920s-style hand-painted carousel in its center court and more than 140 national and regional retailers and restaurants.

**MGM GRAND ADVENTURES THEME PARK** *At the MGM Grand Hotel-Casino, 3799 Las Vegas Blvd. S., 89109. (702) 891-7979. Open daily 10 a.m.-10 p.m. Free admission. Rides: ages 11 and up, $12; ages 2-10 (over 42"), $10.* The 33-acre complex has several major attractions, including a roller coaster, water rides and bumper cars. There are also celebrity look-alikes, strolling performers, musical shows, eight themed areas, restaurants and shops.

**NELLIS AIR FORCE BASE** *Main gate at Las Vegas Blvd. and Craig Rd. (702) 652-1110.* Nellis, a weapons testing and tactical fighter training center, is also the home of the "Thunderbirds," the Air Force's precision flying team. The Thunderbirds are often away performing at air shows throughout the country, but they do perform at the Nellis AFB Open House, which is held every two years; call for schedule.

**Thunderbird Museum** *Located on the base (directions given at main gate). (702) 652-4018. Tours Tue. and Thu. at 2 p.m. Closed last 2 weeks of Dec.* The museum tour is open to the public and features a short program, film and close-up look at an F-16 static display.

**NEVADA STATE MUSEUM AND HISTORICAL SOCIETY** *Located in Lorenzi Park; 700 Twin Lakes Dr., 89107. (702) 486-5205. Open daily 9 a.m.-5 p.m. Closed Jan. 1, Thanksgiving and Dec. 25. Adults, $2; ages 17 and under, free.* This lakeside museum has two main galleries that focus on the history, anthropology and biology of the Southern Nevada region. Another gallery features changing exhibits on important historical, biological or cultural aspects of the area. A research library is also located here. American

Indian jewelry, and books and videos about Nevada's history can be purchased in the museum store.

## NEW YORK NEW YORK HOTEL & CASINO
*3790 Las Vegas Blvd. S., 89109. (702) 740-6969. Manhattan Express roller coaster open daily 10 a.m.-10:30 p.m., Fri.-Sat. to 11 p.m. $4.*
Modeled throughout after its namesake city, New York New York is conspicuous with its 12 Manhattan-style hotel towers, and scale models of the Statue of Liberty and Brooklyn Bridge. Among the main attractions inside is the Coney Island Emporium, an arcade combining an early 1900s atmosphere and old-fashion midway games with the latest high-tech gadgetry. Next to the emporium is the 203-foot-tall Manhattan Express roller coaster.

## OLD LAS VEGAS MORMON FORT STATE HISTORIC PARK
*908 Las Vegas Blvd. N.; State Mail Room, Las Vegas 89158. (702) 486-3511. Call for hours. Donations accepted.* The fort, built by Mormon settlers in 1855, is the oldest European-American building in the state of Nevada. It provided shelter for gold-seekers, emigrants and other travelers along the Spanish Trail/Mormon Road. At the turn-of-the-century, the fort was owned by the San Pedro, Los Angeles and Salt Lake Railroad (now part of Union Pacific); it also served as a resort, dairy and farm for the new, burgeoning town of Las Vegas. Currently, sections of the Old Fort and adjacent ranch buildings are being restored. Historic photographs, interpretive panels and antiques from the mid-1800s are on display at the site.

## OMNIMAX THE-ATRE
*At Caesars Palace, 3570 Las Vegas Blvd. S., 89109. (702) 731-7900. Open daily; showings every 70 minutes*

*New York New York Hotel & Casino, which opened in 1997, is one example of the new wave of theme resorts to open along the Strip in recent years.*

*Sun.-Thu. 2-10 p.m., Fri. and Sat. noon-10:20 p.m.; programs change regularly. Adults, $7; ages 55 and over, military and ages 2-12, $5.* The 368-seat theater contains a movie screen that covers 86 percent of the interior space. Seats recline to a 27-degree angle, allowing the audience an unparalleled view of the screen. The theater has a six-track stereophonic sound system with 16 speaker banks and 86 individual speakers.

**SAHARA PAVILIONS** *Northeast and southeast corners of Sahara Ave. and Decatur Blvd; 4760 W. Sahara #25, 89102. (702) 258-4330. Hours vary by store, some open 24 hours.* This 487,000-square-foot mall has a total of 95 stores, restaurants and services.

**SAM'S TOWN MYSTIC FALLS PARK LASER, LIGHT AND WATER SHOW** *Sam's Town Hotel,* *5111 Boulder Hwy., 89122. (702) 456-7777. Laser show daily at 2, 6, 8 and 10 p.m. Free.* A nine-story atrium encloses this 25,000-square-foot indoor park, which houses lifelike animals, lush tropical foliage, waterfalls and meandering footpaths. Restaurants with patio seating, shops and the hotel itself surround the park. The western-themed laser, light and water show is presented four times daily and features music, laser animation and synchronized show fountains.

**SCANDIA FAMILY FUN CENTER** *On the west side of I-15, south of Sahara Ave.; 2900 Sirius Ave., 89102. (702) 364-0070. Open daily at 10 a.m.; closing times vary. Unlimited all-day wristband, $15.95; Supersaver all-attraction pass, $10.95; or individual ride admissions.* This amusement center features miniature Indy-type race cars,

*Lush tropical foliage, lifelike animals and waterfalls can be found in Sam's Town indoor park.*

*Visible for miles, the Stratosphere Tower defines the northern end of the famous Strip.*

*Scandia Family Fun Center features all kinds of family fun,
including three 18-hole miniature golf courses,
Indy-style racers, bumper boats and a large video game arcade.*

three elaborate 18-hole miniature golf courses, bumper boats, baseball batting cages and a large video game arcade. Snack bar on site.

### SOUTHERN NEVADA ZOOLOGI-CAL-BOTANICAL PARK *3 miles northwest of downtown; 1775 N. Rancho Dr., 89106. (702) 648-5955; 647-4685. Open daily 9 a.m.-4:30 p.m. Closed Jan. 1, Thanksgiving and Dec. 25. Adults, $5; ages 2-12, and 60 and over, $3.* Children will enjoy this small zoological-botanical park, which exhibits a collection of mostly small animals and exotic birds. Featured are the last family of Barbary apes in the U.S., animals ranging from alligators to tigers, and all the venomous reptiles found in Southern Nevada. Birds on display range from talking parrots and ravens to golden eagles and ostrich-

es. A snack bar and gift shop are located on the grounds. Off-road tours of the surrounding desert are also available.

### STRATOSPHERE TOWER *2000 Las Vegas Blvd. S., 89104. (702) 380-7777, (800) 998-6937. Sun.-Thu. 9 a.m.-1 a.m., Fri. and Sat. 9 a.m.-2 a.m. Call for prices and further information.* The focus of the Stratosphere Hotel and Casino is the tower rising 1149 feet above the Strip. The tallest free-standing observation tower in the United States, it is 156 feet taller than the Eiffel Tower in Paris. An eye-catching sight with its futuristic Space Needle-like appearance and soaring height, it features two observation platforms, a revolving restaurant with 360-degree views, cocktail lounge, meeting rooms, two thrill rides (including the world's highest

roller coaster and a free-fall ride), and a retail/entertainment complex.

## UNIVERSITY OF NEVADA, LAS VEGAS

*4505 S. Maryland Pkwy., 89154. (702) 895-3011; campus tours (702) 895-3443.* More than 20,000 students attend classes on the 335-acre campus. The school's curricula include courses in art and architecture, mathematics, engineering, science and a lengthy list of other subjects. The university's first building, Maude Frazier Hall, opened its doors in 1957. After a brief stint as Nevada Southern University, the campus was given autonomy and equality in 1968 with the University of Nevada, Reno, and renamed in 1969. For campus tours, call or drop by the admissions office, Maude Frazier Hall, Room 114. A brochure for the self-guided arboretum tour of the campus is available from the UNLV News and Public Information Office, the Museum of Natural History and the grounds department.

**Artemus W. Ham Concert Hall**, **Judy Bayley Theatre** and **Alta Ham Black Box Theatre** *Adjacent to Maryland Pkwy.; north end of Academic Mall. Schedule and ticket information (702) 895-3801. Tickets range in price from free to $50.* These three facilities form the campus' Performing Arts Center. The center regularly presents major international performing artists in classical and popular music, dance, theater and opera. It is also home to the Nevada Dance Theatre, Nevada Symphony Orchestra, Nevada Opera-

Theatre and the Community Concert Association, whose seasons run from September through May and include professional performances in ballet, symphonic and chamber music, and opera.

**Donna Beam Fine Art Gallery** *In the Alta Ham Fine Arts Bldg., Room 130. Open Mon.-Fri. 8 a.m.-5 p.m. Closed Sat., Sun. and major holidays. Free.* The gallery hosts changing exhibitions by students, faculty and invited artists.

**Flashlight** *Between the Artemus W. Ham Concert Hall and the Judy Bayley Theatre; north end of Academic Mall.* This striking 38-foot-high, 74,000-pound steel sculpture was fashioned by acclaimed artists Claes Oldenberg and Coosje van Bruggen.

**Marjorie Barrick Museum of Natural** *History On campus; east of Swenson St. at end of Harmon Ave. Metered parking adjacent to museum. (702) 895-3381. Open Mon.-Fri. 9 a.m.-4:45 p.m., Sat. 10 a.m.-2 p.m. Closed Sun. and holidays. Free.* The museum encompasses permanent exhibits on the archaeology, geology and biology of the desert Southwest, an outdoor botanical garden and displays of indigenous live animals.

**Sam Boyd Stadium** *Off campus; via US 93/95 (use Russell Rd. exit) in Silver Bowl Regional Park. Ticket information (702) 895-3900.* The stadium is home to the university's NCAA football team, the Rebels, from September through November. It also hosts motocross competitions and concerts in the summer.

**Thomas and Mack Center** *Off Tropicana Ave. at Swenson St. Events schedule and ticket information (702) 895-3900.* This 18,500-seat indoor arena hosts sporting events, concerts and shows. From November through February it is the home court for the school's NCAA Runnin' Rebels Big West basketball team.

**THE VOLCANO** *The Mirage, 3400 Las Vegas Blvd. S., 89109. (702) 791-7111. Shows daily from dusk to midnight. Free.* Located at the hotel's front entrance, the volcano's fiery, smoke-belching explosions occur every few minutes and never fail to momentarily stop traffic on the famous Strip.

**WET 'N WILD** *2601 Las Vegas Blvd. S., 89109. (702) 734-0088. Open May through Sep., daily 10 a.m.-6 p.m.; extended hours Jun., Jul. and Aug. Adults, $23.95; ages 55 and over, $12; ages 3-9, $17.95.* This 26-acre, family-oriented water park features "Willy Willy," a hydra-hurricane ride; "Banzai Banzai," a water roller coaster; and "Bomb Bay," a 76-foot-high water slide. In addition, there are rapids, a 500,000-gallon wave pool, a surf lagoon and a children's pool. There are also areas for sunbathing and picnicking.

**WORLD OF COCA-COLA LAS VEGAS** *In Showcase Mall at 3785 Las Vegas Blvd. S.; 89109. (702) 270-5965, (800) 720-2653. Open daily 10 a.m.-midnight; Fri.-Sat. to 1 a.m. Adults, $4.75; ages 6-12, $2.50.* A museum and bottling plant in one, the World of Coca-Cola immerses visitors in the history and lore surrounding the venerable soft drink. Coca-Cola art, vintage commercials, a life-size soda fountain and free samples are among the attractions. The building's centerpiece is a 100-foot-tall Coke bottle, in which visitors ride to the top to begin the Coca-Cola "experience."

*Wet 'n Wild offers relief from the hot Las Vegas sun.*

*Surrounded by a stark desert land-scape, Floyd Lamb State Park emerges as an oasis of tree-shaded groves and gentle beauty. The park's four small lakes are stocked with rainbow trout in winter and catfish in summer.*

## North Las Vegas

See A Quick Guide to Las Vegas in this chapter under Las Vegas.

**FLOYD LAMB STATE PARK** *15 miles northwest of Las Vegas off US 95; turnoff just southeast of US 157/Kyle Canyon Rd.; 9200 Tule Springs Rd., Las Vegas 89131. (702) 486-5413. Open daily 8 a.m.-dusk. Closed Jan. 1 and Dec. 25. Entrance fee: $5 per vehicle.* The park encompasses 2040 acres, including **Tule Springs Ranch,** four small lakes and the surrounding natural desert area. Fishing is permitted in all four lakes, and all are stocked with rainbow trout in winter and catfish in summer. Largemouth bass live in the lakes, but the catch is low. Swimming, wading and boating are not

allowed. Picnic tables and grills are located throughout the park and are available on a first-come, first-served basis. Self-guided hiking trails traverse tree-shaded groves and pass by the lakes.

The Tule Springs area has long been known as one of the best Pleistocene fossil sites in western North America. Remains found here have included giant sloths, bison, camels, horses and mammoths. Man's first presence in the area, however, only dates back 10,000 to 11,000 years. Today that presence is much more in evidence. The area that is now Floyd Lamb State Park was used as a watering stop by American Indians and local prospectors, and as a rest stop for horses on the Bullfrog Stage Line to Rhyolite. John Herbert Nay began farming the land in 1916, but sold the land in 1928. It remained vacant until 1941 when Jacob Goumond turned it into a working ranch.

## ▼ *Grand Canyon Flights*

In 1987 the U.S. Congress passed a law prohibiting flights below the canyon rim and directed the National Park Service (NPS) and the Federal Aviation Administration (FAA) to designate safe routes for flights over the national park area. The NPS then proposed to the FAA that flight-free zones be established over 40 percent of the Grand Canyon, that air-tour operators be restricted to flying in specific corridors over the least-used parts of the park and that pilots be required to stay above the canyon rim. The law took effect in September 1988. A study is being conducted to assess the impact of these restrictions. According to a government spokesperson, those flying over the canyon can still view much of the grandeur of the park. The main concerns are passenger safety and the level of noise the flights generate. Future guidelines may place limits on the number of flights over the canyon and gradually phase out the noisiest aircraft.

When Nevada's divorce laws became the most liberal in the country by requiring only a six-week residency, Goumond saw a chance to make money with a "dude" ranch. Divorcees who came to live out their residency requirements occupied themselves with horseback riding, swimming, tennis, hayrides, barbecues, dances and a shooting range. But even as a dude ranch, Tule Springs remained a working farm. Livestock included a herd of cattle, dairy cows, horses, chickens, turkeys and pigs.

Fruits and vegetables were grown year round and 100 acres were cultivated in alfalfa. Ranch denizens today include peacocks, ducks and geese. Visitors may roam the grounds of the old Tule Springs Ranch, a group of 22 historic structures currently used only by park staff; future plans call for rehabilitation of the site. The buildings are identified in a park brochure, available at the entrance station.

## GUIDED TOURS

The tours listed in this section generally last less than a day, though some of the trips to more distant places involve an overnight stay. Be sure to contact the companies in advance for complete information and reservations; many tours offer hotel pickup and discounted children's rates. Also, check refund policies to avoid losing your deposit in the event of a late cancellation. Scheduled tours are subject to cancellation if there is an insufficient number of passengers.

*Tours listed are provided as a convenience for our readers; inclusion in this publication does not imply an endorsement by the Automobile Club of Southern California.*

## Henderson

**SIGHTSEEING TOURS UNLIMITED (STU)** *612 S. 3rd St., Las Vegas 89102. (702) 361-3638.* Grand Canyon,

Hoover Dam, Lake Mead, Las Vegas, Laughlin air and land tours.

# Las Vegas

**AIR NEVADA** *McCarran International Airport; P.O. Box 11105, 89111. (702) 736-8900, (800) 634-6377 (outside Nev.).* Daily flights from Las Vegas. Grand Canyon, Bryce Canyon, Monument Valley, Hoover Dam air, land and air/land packages.

**AIR VEGAS AIRLINES** *McCarran International Airport; P.O. Box 11008, 89111. (702) 736-3599, (800) 255-7474; FAX (702) 361-8967.* Grand Canyon, Bryce Canyon, Monument Valley and Hoover Dam air and air/land tours.

**CACTUS JACK'S WILD WEST TOUR COMPANY** *2217 Paradise Rd., Ste. A, 89104. (702) 731-2425; FAX (702) 731-2425.* Grand Canyon, Lake Mead, Hoover Dam, and Laughlin air/land and land tours.

**DESTINATION LAS VEGAS UNLIMITED** *1050 E. Flamingo Rd., 89119. (702) 733-6060; FAX (702) 733-6611.* Grand Canyon, Hoover Dam, Lake Mead, Laughlin air, land and air/land tours.

**EAGLE CANYON AIRLINES** *275 E. Tropicana, Ste. 220, 89109. (702) 740-8300, (800) 446-4584; FAX (702) 736-3333.* Grand Canyon air and land tours.

**FLAG TOURS** *4740 S. Valley View Blvd. # 100, 89103. (702) 798-7077, (888) 267-2007; FAX (702) 798-7066.* Grand Canyon, Colorado River, Hoover Dam/Lake Mead, Las Vegas, Laughlin and Primm land tours.

**GRAY LINE TOURS** *1550 S. Industrial Rd., 89102-2699. (702) 384-1234; FAX (702) 387-6401.* Grand Canyon, Colorado River, Hoover Dam/Lake Mead, Valley of Fire/Lost City Museum of Archeology, Red Rock Canyon/Mount Charleston, Las Vegas, Laughlin land tours and air/land packages.

**INTERSTATE TOURS** *P.O. Box 94105, Las Vegas, 89193. (702) 294-2268, (800) 245-1166.* Grand Canyon, Zion, Death Valley, Hoover Dam, Lake Mead and Colorado River land tours.

**KEY TOURS** *3305 W. Spring Mountain Rd., Ste. 16, 89102. (702) 362-9355.* Hoover Dam, Laughlin and Primm land tours. Departures from the

*Flights over Grand Canyon National Park are popular with Las Vegas visitors.*

Four Queens, Silver City, Flamingo Hilton, Circus Circus, Harrah's, Excalibur and Tropicana hotels.

**RAY AND ROSS TRANSPORT, INC.** *3860 W. Tompkins Ave., 89103. (702) 646-4661, (800) 338-8111 (outside Nev.); FAX (702) 646-3040.* Hoover Dam/Ethel M Chocolates Factory, Lake Mead, Las Vegas, Laughlin land tours and air/land packages. Private charter tours to Grand Canyon.

**SHOWTIME TOURS OF LAS VEGAS** *4699 S. Industrial Rd., Ste. 14, 89103. (702) 895-8822; FAX (702) 895-9366.* Grand Canyon, Hoover Dam, Laughlin air and air/land tours.

**SIGHTSEEING TOURS UNLIM-ITED** *Departure terminal at 1201 Las Vegas Blvd. S.; 612 S. Third St. 89101. (702) 471-7155; FAX (702) 471-7187.* Grand Canyon, Hoover Dam/Lake Mead, Las Vegas city air and land tours.

**SUNDANCE HELICOPTERS, INC.** *265 E. Tropicana., Ste. 130, 89109. (702) 736-0606, (800) 653-1881; FAX (702) 736-4107.* Grand Canyon, Hoover Dam/Lake Mead and Las Vegas helicopter tours.

# North Las Vegas

**SCENIC AIRLINES** *2705 Airport Dr., 89030. (702) 638-3300, (800) 634-*

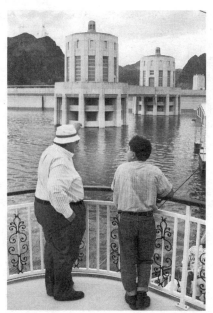

*Majestic Hoover Dam is a popular guided tour destination.*

6801 (outside Nev.); FAX (702) 638-3275. Grand Canyon, Monument Valley, Bryce Canyon, Phoenix, Lake Powell air/land tours.

## SHOWROOM ENTERTAINMENT

Headline entertainment is second only to gambling in the number of visitors it attracts to Las Vegas. The big showrooms feature either a well-known singer or comedian backed by an opening act, or a glitzy production number with elaborate sets and costumes. Facilities listed here seat 500 or more. Showroom listing does not imply AAA endorsement for the lodging establishment. For the most current information, refer to the Auto Club's Las Vegas Shows schedule, available to AAA members at all district offices.

Tickets for production shows can be purchased by phoning or visiting the hotel's showroom box office or by contacting a local ticket agency. There are a number of ticket agencies in Las Vegas that specialize in booking entertainment. Refer to the telephone directory yellow pages under "Ticket Sales/Events" or "Tourist Information."

Many showrooms offer advance ticket sales and reserved seating. Be sure to ask at the time of purchase if the seats are reserved. If you have assigned seats you should arrive about 20 minutes prior to show time. If seats are not assigned, then it is advisable to arrive at least an hour prior to curtain. As for dinner shows, remember that the time given is performance time. You should arrive at the theater about two hours early for a dinner performance.

The prices listed for each show may not include the 7 percent sales tax, 10 percent entertainment tax or any gratuities. In addition to these extra charges, the prices will often be raised for some especially popular entertainers, as well as for opening and closing nights.

Large production shows often run indefinitely, many of them for several years. As of press time, shows scheduled to run indefinitely appear in the listings, but **any show is subject to change without notice. You are advised to verify shows, times and prices in advance.**

Although the early and late shows are basically the same in terms of content, children are not admitted to the late shows. The hour alone prevents most children from enjoying themselves, and entertainers like to feel freer to use language and discuss subjects that might not be appropriate for a general audience. For this reason, not only children

*Elaborate stage productions entertain thousands of visitors with dazzling sets and beautiful dancers.*

but sensitive adults should attend the early shows. Production shows with nude performers usually do not admit children; call the theater's box office in advance for any age restrictions that may apply. Hotels housing showrooms are not necessarily AAA-approved accommodations.

# Las Vegas

**BALLY'S LAS VEGAS**
*3645 Las Vegas Blvd. S. (702) 739-4567.*

**Celebrity Room** — Top-name entertainment. *Times and prices vary with entertainers.*

**Jubilee Theatre** — "Jubilee" (Indefinitely). *Sat.-Thu. 8 and 11 p.m., except Sun. and Mon. 8 p.m. only. Dark Fri. $49.50-66 per person. Minimum age 18.*

**CAESARS PALACE**
*3570 Las Vegas Blvd. S. (702) 731-7333.*

**Circus Maximus** — Top-name entertainment. *Times and prices vary with entertainers. Minimum age 6. Tickets can be purchased 60-90 days in advance by phone.*

**DEBBIE REYNOLDS HOLLYWOOD HOTEL**
*305 Convention Center Dr. (702) 733-2243.*

**Debbie's Star Theatre** — "The Debbie Reynolds Show" (Indefinitely). *Tue.-Fri. 8 p.m., call for show time. Dark Sun. and Mon. $39.95 per person.*

"The Kenny Kerr Show" (Indefinitely). *Mon.-Sat., call for show time. Dark Sun. $21.95 per person. Minimum age 18.*

## THE DESERT INN
*3145 Las Vegas Blvd. S. (702) 733-4566.*

**Crystal Room** — Top-name entertainment. *Times and prices vary with entertainers. Smoke-free theater.*

## EXCALIBUR HOTEL & CASINO
*3850 Las Vegas Blvd. S. (800) 933-1334, (702) 597-7600.*

**King Arthur's Arena** — "King Arthur's Tournament" (Indefinitely). *Nightly dinner shows at 6 and 8:30 p.m. $29.95 per person. Tickets can be purchased 6 days in advance by phone or at box office.*

## FLAMINGO HILTON-LAS VEGAS
*3555 Las Vegas Blvd. S. (702) 733-3111, 733-3333.*

**Flamingo Showroom** — "The Great Radio City Music Hall Spectacular, Starring the Rockettes" (Indefinitely). *Sat.-Thu. Dark Fri. Dinner show: 7:45 p.m., from $49.50 per person. Show only: 10:30 p.m., $42.50 per person.*

## HARD ROCK HOTEL AND CASINO
*4455 Paradise Rd. (702) 226-4650.*

**The Joint** — Top-name entertainment. *Times and prices vary with entertainers. Tickets also sold at hotel box office and through Ticketmaster.*

## HARRAH'S-LAS VEGAS
*3475 Las Vegas Blvd. S. (702) 369-5222.*

**Commander's Theatre** — "Spellbound—Starring Mark Kalin and Jinger" (Indefinitely). *Mon.-Sat. 7:30*

*Good battles evil in Excalibur's knightly dinner spectacular,*
*"King Arthur's Tournament."*

and 10 p.m. Dark Sun. $39.10 per person. Minimum age 5.

## IMPERIAL PALACE
*3535 Las Vegas Blvd. S. (702) 794-3261.*

**Imperial Theatre** — "Legends in Concert" (Indefinitely). *Mon.-Sat. 7:30 and 10:30 p.m. Dark Sun. $29.50 per person; ages 11 and under, $14.75. Smoke-free theater.*

## LAS VEGAS HILTON
*3000 Paradise Rd. (702) 732-5755.*

**Hilton Showroom** — Top-name entertainment. *Times and prices vary with entertainers.*

## MGM GRAND HOTEL CASINO
*3799 Las Vegas Blvd. S. (800) 929-1111, (702) 891-7777.*

**Hollywood Theatre** — *Top-name entertainment. Times and prices vary with entertainers.*

**MGM Grand Garden Arena** — Top-name entertainment/special events. *Times and prices vary with entertainers.*

**MGM Grand Theatre** — "EFX! Starring David Cassidy" (Indefinitely). *Tue.-Sat. 7:30 and 10:30 p.m. Dark Sun. and Mon. $45-64 per person.*

## THE MIRAGE
*3400 Las Vegas Blvd. S. (702) 791-7111, 792-7777.*

**Siegfried and Roy Theatre** — "Siegfried and Roy at the Mirage" (Indefinitely). *Fri.-Tue. 7:30 and 11 p.m. Dark Wed. and Thu. $83.85 per person. Minimum age 5. Tickets can be purchased 3 days in advance.*

## MONTE CARLO RESORT & CASINO
*3770 Las Vegas Blvd. S. (702) 730-7000, (800) 311-8999.*

**Lance Burton Theatre** — "Lance Burton, Master Magician" (Indefinitely). *Tue.-Sat. 7:30 and 10:30 p.m. Dark Sun. and Mon. $34.95-39.95 per person.*

## NEW YORK NEW YORK HOTEL & CASINO
*3790 Las Vegas Blvd. S. (702) 740-6969.*

**The Madhattan Theatre** — "Madhattan" (Indefinitely). *Tue.-Sun. 7:30 and 10 p.m. Dark Mon. $40 per person.*

## THE ORLEANS
*4500 W. Tropicana Ave. (702) 365-7075.*

**Branson Theatre** — Top-name entertainment. *Times and prices vary with entertainers.*

## RIO SUITE HOTEL & CASINO
*3700 Flamingo Rd. (702) 252-7777.*

**Copacabana Showroom** — *"Danny Gans: The Man of Many Voices"* (Indefinitely). *Wed.-Sun. 8 p.m. Dark Mon. and Tue. $60 per person.*

## RIVIERA HOTEL
*2901 Las Vegas Blvd. S. (702) 794-9433 (Mardi Gras Plaza); (702) 794-9301 (Versailles Theatre).*

**Mardi Gras Plaza** — "An Evening at La Cage" (Indefinitely). *Wed.-Mon. 7:30 and 9:30 p.m., additional 11:15 p.m. show Wed. and Sat. Dark Tue. Show and buffet: $33.08-38.58 per person. Show only: $22.66-32.16 per person.*

**Versailles Theatre** — "Splash II"
(Indefinitely). *Nightly 7:30 and 10:30
p.m. $45.58-56.45 per person. Minimum
age 18.*

**SAHARA HOTEL**
*2535 Las Vegas Blvd. S. (702) 737-2111.*

**Congo Room** —Top-name entertainment. *Times and prices vary with entertainers. Smoke-free theater.*

**STARDUST HOTEL**
*3000 Las Vegas Blvd. S. (800) 824-6033,
(702) 732-6325.*

**Stardust Theatre** — "Enter the Night"
(Indefinitely). *Tue.-Thu. and Sat. 7:30
and 10:30 p.m., Sun. and Mon. 8 p.m.
Dark Fri. $26.90 per person.*

*Cirque du Soleil is famous
for its cutting-edge acrobatics, unusual
music and old European theatrics.*

**STRATOSPHERE HOTEL
& CASINO**
*2000 Las Vegas Blvd. S. (702) 380-7777,
(800) 998-6937.*

**Broadway Showroom** — "American
Superstars" (Indefinitely*). Fri.-Wed. 7
and 10 p.m. Dark Thursday. $22.95 per
person.*

"Viva Las Vegas" (Indefinitely). *Mon.-
Sat. 2 and 4 p.m. Dark Sun. $11 per
person.*

**TREASURE ISLAND AT THE
MIRAGE**
*3300 Las Vegas Blvd. S. (702) 894-7722,
(800) 392-1999.*

**Treasure Island Showroom** —
"Cirque du Soleil—Mystère"
(Indefinitely). *Wed.-Sun. 7:30 and
10:30 p.m. Dark Mon. and Tues. $64.90
per person; children ages 11 and under,
$32.45. Tickets can be purchased 7 days
in advance by phone.*

**TROPICANA RESORT AND
CASINO**
*3801 Las Vegas Blvd. S. (702) 739-2411,
(800) 468-9494.*

**Tiffany Theatre** — "Folies Bergere"
(Indefinitely). *Sun.-Thu. and selected
Fri. 7:30 and 10:30 p.m. Dark Sat.
Dinner show: $45-55 per person.
Minimum age 16.*

## ANNUAL EVENTS

Parades, rodeos, art fairs, fireworks displays and golf tournaments are just a
few of the many annual community
events that Las Vegas and environs have
to offer. For detailed information about
each event, please call the telephone
numbers shown or consult with the
local chamber of commerce or visitor
information bureau. In addition, casino
tournaments take place throughout the
year, and in Las Vegas spectator sports
range from boxing to baseball, soccer
to football and basketball to hockey.

**Spectator sports** are popular throughout the year in the Las Vegas area. The Las Vegas Stars baseball club (702-386-7200), affiliated with the San Diego Padres of the National League, plays its home games at Cashman Field April through September. The Thomas & Mack Center is the home of two teams: the International Hockey League's Las Vegas Thunder (702-798-7825), from October through April; and UNLV's NCAA Big West basketball team, the Runnin' Rebels (702-895-3900), who play November through February. Sam Boyd Stadium is the home venue for Rebels university football; the season runs September through November.

Auto racing is a fast-growing sport at the Las Vegas Motor Speedway, which hosts the Las Vegas 400 NASCAR race in March and many other events throughout the year. For more information, call (702) 644-4444. Other exciting sporting events throughout the year include AWA wrestling competitions at the Showboat Hotel; WBA and WBC boxing matches at the Las Vegas Hilton, Caesars Palace and MGM Grand hotels; and ESPN Top Rank boxing matches at Bally's Casino Resort.

**Casino tournaments** in bridge, blackjack, slot play, craps, poker, gin rummy and bowling take place in many casinos. Anyone interested in these tournaments should contact the hotel or venue directly for dates and play information; room reservations should be made well in advance, as room space is often at a premium during a tournament.

## February

**LAS VEGAS INTERNATIONAL MARATHON** *Starting point in Jean, Nev. (702) 876-3870.* The marathon, which finishes in the parking lot of Vacation Village in Las Vegas, was run for the 31st time in 1997. An additional attraction is the half-marathon, which starts in Sloan, Nev., and finishes at Vacation Village. Each event attracts more than 6000 participants.

*On your mark, get set, go! Runners take to the streets in the Las Vegas International Marathon.*

## March

**FLYING COLORS KITE EXPO**
*Silver Bowl Sports Complex, Las Vegas,*
*Nev. (702) 455-8206.* This one-day
event offers free kite workshops,
demonstrations and contests for all
ages.

## April

**EARTH FAIR** *Sunset Park, Las Vegas,*
*Nev. (702) 642-3333.* This fair celebrates Earth Day and the environment
with exhibits, informational booths,
music and entertainment.

**HENDERSON HERITAGE**
**DAYS** *Various locations, Henderson,*
*Nev. (702) 565-8951.* This 10-day
event celebrates Henderson's heritage
with a chili cookoff, car show, baseball
tournament, street dances and parade.

**LAS VEGAS SENIOR CLASSIC**
*Tournament Players Club at The*
*Canyons, Summerlin, Nev. (702) 382-*
*6616.* This event is a three-day PGA
senior golf tournament.

**NATIVE AMERICAN ARTS**
**FESTIVAL** *Clark County Heritage*
*Museum, Henderson, Nev. (702) 455-*
*7955.* Native American food and art,
dancing, craft demonstrations and
storytelling are featured during this
three-day festival.

## May

**HELLDORADO DAYS, RODEO**
**AND PARADE** *Thomas & Mack*
*Center, Las Vegas, Nev. (702) 870-1221.*
*Some years takes place in Jun.* This four-
day event commemorates Las Vegas'
western heritage with a PRCA rodeo.

**CRAFT FAIR AND RIB**
**BURN-OFF** *Sunset Park, Las Vegas,*

*Nev. (702) 455-8206.* Craft booths,
barbecue, live music and children's
activities round out the festivities during this two-day event.

## June

**KKLZ JUNEFEST** *Silver Bowl Park,*
*Las Vegas, Nev. (702) 739-9600.* Classic
rock bands perform at the park on the
first Saturday of the month.

## July

**FOURTH OF JULY FESTIVITIES**
*Thomas & Mack Center, Las Vegas,*
*Nev. (702) 895-3900; Sam Boyd's Silver*
*Bowl, Henderson, Nev. (702) 895-3900.*
Traditional celebrations and fireworks
mark Independence Day.

## September

**LAS VEGAS MARIACHI**
**FESTIVAL** *Las Vegas, Nev. (800)*
*637-1006.* This one-day mariachi festival is one of the most prestigious of its
kind in the U.S. Formerly held at the
Aladdin Hotel & Casino, the festival
moves to the Thomas & Mack Center
in 1998.

## October

**HENDERSON EXPO** *Convention*
*Center, Henderson, Nev. (702) 565-*
*8951.* A home show, food booths
and carnival round out this three-day
event.

**LAS VEGAS BALLOON CLASSIC**
*Silver Bowl Park, Las Vegas, Nev. (702)*
*434-0848.* Hot air balloons compete
for the Nevada "Silver State"
Championship during this three-day
event. Craft booths, food and entertainment are featured.

**LAS VEGAS INVITATIONAL GOLF TOURNAMENT** *Desert Inn Golf Club, Las Vegas Country Club and TPC at Summerlin. (702) 242-3000.* This PGA tour event is five days long.

**LAS VEGAS JAYCEES STATE FAIR** *Cashman Field, Las Vegas, Nev. (702) 457-8832. Sometimes held in Sep.* Livestock exhibits, a carnival midway and crafts booths are featured at this six-day event.

**RENAISSANCE FAIRE** *Sunset Park, Las Vegas, Nev. (702) 455-8200.* Historical re-enactments, jousting, theatrical performances, food and strolling minstrels highlight this two-day event.

## November

**ITT-LPGA TOUR CHAMPI-ONSHIP** *Desert Inn Golf Club, Las Vegas, Nev. (888) 254-4653.* Top women's professional golfers on the LPGA Tour compete in this week-long event.

## December

**CHILDREN'S CHRISTMAS PARADE** *Water St., Henderson, Nev. (702) 565-8951.* Held on a Saturday, this parade features floats, horses and a visit from Santa Claus.

**NATIONAL FINALS RODEO** *UNLV's Thomas & Mack Center, Las Vegas, Nev. (702) 731-2115, 895-3900.* This professional rodeo event takes place over 10 days and features saddle bronco, bareback and bull riding; calf roping; steer wrestling; and barrel racing.

**NEW YEAR'S EVE CELEBRA-TIONS** *Various locations. (702) 892-7575.*

**USA NATIONAL TABLE TENNIS CHAMPIONSHIPS** *Las Vegas Convention Center. (719) 578-4583.* Table tennis players compete over five days in divisions ranging from Men's and Women's Singles to Elementary Boys and Girls.

**WINTER WONDERLAND** *Sunset Park, Las Vegas, Nev. (702) 455-8200.* The winter season is celebrated with a day of reindeer games, ice carving demonstrations, snow play (weather permitting) and live entertainment.

*The National Finals Rodeo brings PRCA events to the Thomas & Mack Center in Las Vegas.*

# Outside Las Vegas

*From the grandeur of Hoover Dam to the pine forests of Mount Charleston, a world of opportunities beckons those who venture beyond the neon lights and go-go atmosphere of Las Vegas. Most of the surrounding region remains undeveloped, with a host of opportunities awaiting the adventurous traveler. To the southeast of Las Vegas is* **Boulder City**, *a tidy town that has maintained its down-home, historic atmosphere. The town serves as gateway to Hoover Dam and the many diversions of Lake Mead National Recreation Area. For breathtaking desert views, head west to Red Rock National Conservation Area or northeast to Valley of Fire State Park, both within an hour's drive of the Strip. Close as well is Spring Mountains National Recreation Area, home of Mount Charleston, the third-highest peak in Nevada. It's less than an hour's drive to the northwest. At the California-Nevada border, the tiny town of* **Primm** *has emerged as a family entertainment center. Thanks to the "Desperado" roller-coaster and other thrill rides, this former drive-through has become a tourist destination in its own right.*

## POINTS OF INTEREST

Attractions are listed alphabetically by city or area – **Boulder City**, **Lake Mead National Recreation Area**, **Overton**, **Primm**, **Red Rock Canyon National Conservation Area**, **Spring Mountains National Recreation Area** and **Valley of Fire State Park**. Listings in this chapter of attractions located on hotel properties do not necessarily imply AAA approval of the lodging facilities.

See A Quick Guide to Las Vegas and Vicinity in the *Las Vegas Valley* chapter for information on the areas included in this chapter.

## Boulder City

**BOULDER CITY HISTORIC DISTRICT** *23 miles southeast of Las Vegas via US 93/95 on US 93/Nevada Hwy.* **Chamber of Commerce** *located at 1305 Arizona St., 89005. (702) 293-2034.* Boulder City was created to house the thousands of workers who built nearby Hoover Dam. It also takes a place in American history as this

country's first fully developed, master-planned community. Listed on the National Register of Historic Places, Boulder City provides a glimpse into an earlier era, an oasis of Americana in the vast Southern Nevada desert.

Among Boulder City's many historic buildings, visitors will encounter numerous parks, generous landscaping, wide avenues lined with vintage street lamps and charming, well-kept homes. Interestingly, this community of 14,460 is also the only city in Nevada where gaming has always been, and still is, illegal.

The construction of Boulder City began in 1931 and continued nonstop for nearly two years. While the rest of the country struggled during the Great Depression, this sparkling new community thrived—the population swelled to more than 8000 while the dam was being built. At that time Boulder City was the third largest city in Nevada.

Through the 1940s, Boulder City flourished as a regional government center and tourism point for the dam and Lake

Mead. However, the community remained under the jurisdiction of the federal government, ensuring its proper development under the original plan. It took an act of Congress for Boulder City to become an incorporated municipality. The act passed and was signed on July 9, 1958, and Boulder City was incorporated on January 4, 1960.

A self-guided tour of the Boulder City Historic District is outlined in a brochure available at the local chamber of commerce. The historic district is divided into five major areas, including parks and public buildings, three residential sections and a commercial district. The city's best-known historic structure and focal point is the **Boulder Dam Hotel**, a pine-shingled, Dutch Colonial-style building on Arizona Street. Built in 1933 to accommodate a growing tourist industry, the 33-room hotel was Southern Nevada's finest inn, boasting private baths and showers in each room—a rarity for the times—and an elegant lobby paneled in rare southern gumwood. The hotel hosted a steady stream of Hollywood celebrities, American politicians, European aristocrats and Far Eastern royalty. Currently, the Boulder Dam Hotel is undergoing a full restoration and will soon be the new home of the Boulder City Chamber of Commerce, the Boulder City/Hoover Dam Museum, and the Boulder City Arts Council and Art Gallery. The restoration is due for completion in 1999.

**BOULDER CITY/HOOVER DAM MUSEUM** *444 Hotel Plaza; P.O. Box 60516, 89006. (702) 294-1988. Open daily 10 a.m.-4 p.m. Closed Jan. 1, Thanksgiving and Dec. 25. $1 donation.* This small museum exhibits Hoover Dam-related artifacts, including a display of a dam workers' tent-house and a variety of historical photographs.

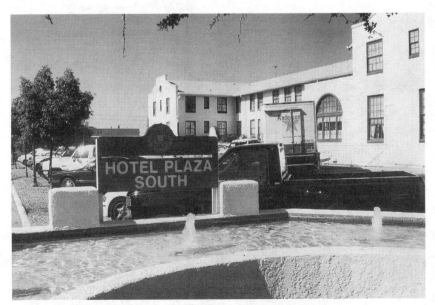

*The Boulder City Historic District preserves the atmosphere of an earlier era.*

TO KINGMAN

93

68

SEE LAUGHLIN AND
BULLHEAD CITY MAP

ARIZONA

BULLHEAD CITY

TEMPLE BAR

95

*River*

LAUGHLIN

WILLOW
BEACH

MOUNTAIN
TIME

Grapevine Canyon

163

WILLOW BEACH
HARBOR

PACIFIC
TIME

*Colorado*

COTTONWOOD
COVE RESORT
AND MARINA

*Lake
Mohave*

COTTONWOOD
COVE

CHRISTMAS TREE
PASS

TO NEEDLES

95

SEARCHLIGHT

164

Reproduction of this map or
any portion thereof constitutes
infringement of copyright.

NEVADA

CALIFORNIA

JEAN

15

PRIMM

BUFFALO BILL'S RESORT & CASINO
AND THE DESPERADO

PRIMADONNA RESORT
& CASINO & RV VILLAGE

WHISKEY PETE'S
HOTEL & CASINO

MONORAIL
ROUTE

PRIMM VALLEY GOLF CLUB

TO HOOVER DAM

VILLE DR

ARIZONA ST.
BOULDER CITY/
HOOVER DAM MUS.

BEST WESTERN
LIGHTHOUSE INN

BOULDER
CITY
CHAMBER OF COMMERCE /
BOULDER DAM HOTEL

CLUBHOUSE DR

BOULDER CITY
GOLF COURSE

EL RANCHO BOULDER MOTEL /
SANDS MOTEL

ELM ST.

NEVADA

BUCHANAN

BOULDER THEATER

BOULDER CITY

93

BOULDER CITY
AIRPORT

TO LAUGHLIN

MAP 2773

93
95

95

TO LAUGHLIN

BOULDER
CITY

TO BARSTOW

## LAS VEGAS REGION

- ◢◖ FREEWAY & ACCESS RAMPS
- ▬ PAVED ROAD
- ▭ UNPAVED ROAD
- ◉ POINT OF INTEREST
- ○ GOLF COURSE
- ▢ AAA APPROVED
  HOTEL OR MOTEL
- ● CAMPGROUND
- ▲ BOATING FACILITY
- ▫ MISCELLANEOUS RECREATION

SCALE IN MILES

0     5     10

**BOULDER THEATER** *1225 Arizona St., 89005. Movie information, (702) 293-3145; tour information, (702) 293-6982. First-run movies shown daily; call for schedule and prices. Tours available by arrangement, $3.* Opened in 1932, the Boulder Theater is the oldest movie theater in continuous operation in Nevada. The building is listed in the National Register of Historic Places. A 28-minute movie, consisting of film clips from the town's early days, is projected for groups touring the building.

# Lake Mead National Recreation Area

**HOOVER DAM** *30 miles southeast of Las Vegas via US 93/95 on US 93; P.O. Box 60400, Boulder City 89006. (702) 294-3523. Guided tours daily; Apr.-Oct. from 8:30 a.m.-5:30 p.m.; Nov.-Mar. from 9 a.m.-5 p.m. Closed Dec. 25. Adults, $6; ages 62 and over, $5; ages 6-16, $2; ages 5 and under, free. Hard hat tour $25. Free parking on Ariz. side; paid parking in shelter on Nev. side.* This 726-foot-high dam is a National Historic Landmark and considered one of the engineering wonders of the world. Built during the Great Depression with the skill, long hours and dedication of thousands of construction workers, it was completed in 1935—two years ahead of schedule. Not only did the dam help control the sometimes violent Colorado River, but it provided a cheap source of electricity, which aided the development of Las Vegas and Southern California. As an additional bonus, the dam created Lake Mead, America's largest manmade reservoir and a popular recreation spot.

In 1995, a new $123-million visitor center and five-story parking structure opened to the public. The three-level visitor center features an exhibit gallery, revolving theater and observation platform. Two high-speed elevators operate daily to lower visitors 520 feet into the walls of Black Canyon for a 35-minute tour of the dam's power plant; a one-hour hard hat tour provides a "behind-the-scenes" view of the structure's inner workings. For all visitors, the view from the bottom of Hoover Dam is awesome, leaving no doubt that this structure is truly an engineering marvel.

**LAKE MEAD** *25 miles southeast of Las Vegas.* **Alan Bible Visitor Center** *located 4 miles northeast of Boulder City on US 93. (702) 293-8990, 293-8906. The visitor center is open daily 8:30 a.m. to 4:30 p.m. Closed Jan. 1, Thanksgiving and Dec. 25. Free. The six major recreation areas on Lake Mead are* **Boulder Beach,** *28 miles southeast via US 93 and SR 166;* **Las Vegas Bay,** *17 miles east via SR 147/Lake Mead Blvd.;* **Callville Bay,** *29 miles east via SR 147, Northshore and Callville Bay rds.;* **Echo Bay,** *54 miles northeast via SR 147, Northshore Rd. and access road to Echo Bay;* **Overton Beach,** *60 miles northeast via I-15 and SR 169; and* **Temple Bar,** *in Ariz., 75 miles southeast via US 93 and Temple Bar Rd. For emergency assistance, contact a ranger or call the 24-hour emergency phone number, (702) 293-8932.*

Lake Mead is the largest manmade reservoir in the United States. It is administered by the National Park Service as part of the Lake Mead National Recreation Area, which also includes Lake Mohave downstream from Hoover Dam. Lake Mead measures 110 miles long and has a shoreline five times that length. Created by

Hoover Dam, the lake area offers year-round fishing, swimming, water-skiing, camping, hiking, picnicking, scuba diving, sailing, powerboating and houseboating. Information about the recreation area can be obtained at the Alan Bible Visitor Center on US 93, which also has a botanical garden, bookstore and exhibits on natural history.

Much of Lake Mead's surrounding landscape is rugged desert interspersed with stark grayish-purple mountains, colorful red rock canyons and a variety of desert shrubbery. Mild weather throughout most of the year is punctuated by hot, dry summers when temperatures often reach over 100 degrees. The desert environment is home to more than 1000 bighorn sheep that roam the rocky ridges, while the manmade lake attracts ducks, cormorants, geese, egrets, herons, ospreys and bald eagles.

The lake offers some of the best sportfishing in the country and an open season on all fish year round (see Water Recreation in the *Recreation* chapter).

There are many **scenic drives** through this dramatic region. A popular one follows Northshore Road, running north from Lake Mead Boulevard (SR 147) to Echo Bay and Overton Beach. An often spectacular view of the surrounding mountains and hills can be seen from this route, where the browns, burnt reds and black rocks of the landscape are contrasted with the stark off-whites and tans. Each hill is seemingly formed from a different material, but all are the product of an active geologic past.

The red and black rocks that dominate the scenery speak of the high iron and magnesium content of the volcanic debris. The local sedimentary rocks, such as the sandstone layers evidenced in the nearby hills, were laid down by water and then uplifted at a later time. A high iron content is also evidenced there, often by an entire range of stark red hills. The vividness of the colors of the rocks seen on this drive can often vary not only with the time of day, but also with the direction of travel. What may appear dull and drab through the front

*The 726-foot-high Hoover Dam is considered one of the engineering wonders of the world.*

windshield may look entirely different in the rearview mirror. Drive carefully—the greatest hazard here is looking at the landscape instead of the road.

*Caution:* Care should be taken when traveling in this area.

• Desert thunderstorms in summer and fall can produce both lightning and flash floods. Never camp in a wash or low-lying area. Never drive across flooded roads; many roads have been posted flash-flood areas.

• Summer's extreme temperatures can cause heat exhaustion and heat stroke, as well as cripple a car that does not have adequate coolant in the cooling system. Refer to the Desert Driving Hints in the *Transportation* chapter.

• Rattlesnakes and scorpions are indigenous to this area and poisonous. They usually will not strike unless cornered, but caution should be taken to avoid them.

• Drive only on paved roads or on unpaved roads marked with yellow arrows. Check with rangers about road conditions before traveling unpaved roads.

**LAKE MEAD STATE FISH HATCHERY** *9½ miles north of Boulder City on SR 166/Lakeshore Rd. (702) 486-6738. Open daily 8 a.m.-4 p.m. Free.* This facility is a cold-water hatchery used for trout. Its visitor center features displays on production methods.

**LAKE MOHAVE** *Extends 67 miles north from Davis Dam along the Colorado River. Ranger stations can be found at the three major recreation areas on the lake:* **Katherine Landing**, *6 miles north of Bullhead City via SR 95, SR 68 and north on an access road. (520) 754-3272;* **Cottonwood Cove**, *54 miles north of Laughlin via Laughlin Cutoff Rd., SR 163, US 95 and an access road east from Searchlight. (702) 297-1229; and* **Willow Beach**, *81 miles north of Bullhead City via SR 95, SR 68 to Kingman, US 93 north and an access road west. (520) 767-4000.*

Lake Mohave's teal waters provide a sharp contrast to the desert landscape surrounding it. Its northern section is almost as narrow as the Colorado River itself, with Indian petroglyphs etched on the steep walls of Black Canyon. The midsection widens to almost four miles before narrowing again to the south, where the shore is lined with hundreds of small coves and inlets.

The contrast of the water to the desert is also reflected in the colorful flora and fauna. In all, there are some 60 species of mammals in the area. The desert provides a home for Gila monsters, scorpions, tarantulas, burros and coyotes; the lake attracts small beavers, muskrats and bighorn sheep. Birds run the gamut from hawks and large crows to roadrunners and blue heron. Spring often brings a display of wildflowers (most notably brittlebush and sand verbena) among the desert plants.

Lake Mohave is ideal for boating year round, but those pursuing land adventures will find the best months to visit are October through April. Winters are mild, with daytime temperatures generally ranging from 65 to 85 degrees. Brutally hot summers are routinely above the 100-degree mark and sometimes reach 120 degrees.

The lake's main appeal is in the variety of recreation it offers. Houseboating and fishing are popular, as are swimming, scuba diving, water-skiing, wind surfing, jet skiing and sunbathing. Houseboats can be rented at Katherine Landing and Cottonwood Cove marinas, but reservations must be made well in advance. A fish hatchery at Willow Beach supplies the rainbow trout that are planted in the lake. Lake Mohave has a reputation as one of the best trout and largemouth bass fishing areas in the Southwest.

# Overton

**LOST CITY MUSEUM OF ARCHEOLOGY** *60 miles northeast of Las Vegas via I-15 and SR 169; 721 S. Moapa Valley Blvd.; P.O. Box 807, 89040. (702) 397-2193. Open daily 8:30 a.m.-4:30 p.m. Closed major holidays. Adults, $2; ages 17 and under, free.* This museum offers visitors a chance to see both original American Indian relics and faithful reconstructions of Pueblo dwellings. The last 10,000 years have seen several cultures in residence, including the Gypsum Cave People, Ancient Basketmakers, Early Pueblos and most recently, the Paiute Indians who came to the area about 900 years ago. Many ruins near the museum have not yet been excavated, and as the delicate process of unearthing the remains continues, more and more is revealed about the past inhabitants of the area.

*Faithful reconstructions of Indian pueblo dwellings can be found at the Lost City Museum of Archeology in Overton.*

# Primm

*Located 40 miles south of Las Vegas at the California/Nevada state line on I-15, 89019. Buffalo Bill's, Primadonna and Whiskey Pete's (702) 382-1212, (800) 386-7867. Roller coaster and Turbo Drop, $5 per person; log ride, $4 per person; motion theater, $3 per person.* This area, quite literally at the California-Nevada state line, was once just a drive-through on the way to bigger and better things. It was popularly known as Stateline for several years. Today, however, Primm is itself a high-wattage destination, offering entertainment, lodging, dining and gaming at three large resort-style hotels.

At Buffalo Bill's Resort & Casino, the tallest and fastest roller coaster in the U.S., the **"Desperado,"** offers thrilling rides around the entire property and into the casino itself. The roller coaster plunges 225 feet and reaches speeds of 80 mph while riders glimpse spectacular views of the surrounding desert.

Additional thrills can be had on the **Turbo Drop**, which lifts riders 200 feet above the desert and sends them down at 45 mph before bouncing gently on air brakes. A little tamer, but just as fun, is the **Water Flume Log Ride**, which crisscrosses the path of the roller coaster and finishes with a gentle ride through the casino.

A **western-style train** links Buffalo Bill's to the Primadonna Resort & Casino, where visitors can enjoy a free ride on the 100-foot **Ferris wheel**, hop on the **merry-go-round** or hit a few strikes in the regulation **bowling center**. The Primadonna also touts a brand-new, 21,000-square-foot **convention center**.

From the Primadonna, a sleek, futuristic-looking **monorail** whisks passengers over the I-15 to Whiskey Pete's Hotel & Casino. The hotel displays two classic gangster cars near the monorail terminal: the **original Bonnie and Clyde "Death Car"** and the restored **Dutch Shultz-Al Capone Gangster Car**.

*Primm is the site of a growing number of attractions.*

Meanwhile, Primm has shown no signs of standing pat as it continues to add new attractions. In 1997 the **Primm Valley Golf Club** opened, offering two 18-hole championship courses to guests at Primm's three hotels. (See Golf in the *Recreation* chapter.) The Turbo Drop and convention center were also new additions during 1997. Looking ahead, the first phase of a planned million-square-foot mall, the **Fashion Outlet of Las Vegas**, is scheduled to open in the summer of 1998. The mall will feature upscale stores from apparel companies around the world, a food court, a virtual reality arcade and at least one thrill ride.

# Red Rock Canyon National Conservation Area

*18 miles west of Las Vegas via SR 159/W. Charleston Blvd. or 20 miles west of Las Vegas via SR 160/Blue Diamond Rd.* **Visitor center** *located to the left of the scenic loop drive entrance; mailing address: Bureau of Land Management, Red Rock Canyon National Conservation Area, HCR 33, Box 5500, Las Vegas 89124. (702) 363-1921. Open daily 8:30 a.m.-4:30 p.m. Closed Thanksgiving and Dec. 25. Entrance fee: $5 per vehicle; bicyclists and pedestrians free.* Just a short drive from the urban wonders of Las Vegas, Red Rock Canyon features nature at its best: a 13-mile scenic loop drive, more than 20 miles of hiking trails, horseback riding, numerous panoramic overlooks, a variety of flora and fauna, American Indian rock art, plus a well-stocked visitor center with exhibit rooms and a bookstore. Picnicking sites are located at Red Spring and Willow Spring.

Because Red Rock Canyon is higher in elevation than Las Vegas (up to 5000 feet) and has double the annual rainfall (about 8 to 12 inches), a wider variety of plant and animal life is able to flourish here. Cacti, annuals, agave (such as the Joshua tree) and trees (ponderosa and piñon pines, juniper and willow) are prevalent, as are many types of birds, such as hawks, eagles, falcons, roadrunners, owls, ravens and wrens. Many other birds migrate through during the spring and fall; the visitor center staff can provide a complete list.

Much of the wildlife in Red Rock is visible only during the early morning and late evening hours, when cooler temperatures prevail. Night-dwellers include mule deer, coyotes, mountain lions, badgers, bobcats, jack rabbits and bats. Easier-to-spot daytimers are bighorn sheep, wild burros, wild horses and antelope ground squirrels (identified by their white tails).

Reptiles are no strangers to the area, and include tree frogs, geckos, lizards and snakes. There are also three types of poisonous rattlesnakes here, namely the sidewinder, Mojave green and Mojave speckled. Hot days (above 70 degrees) bring out snakes; use caution when hiking. And remember, all animals (including snakes) are protected at Red Rock Canyon.

The **Scenic Loop Drive** is a convenient way to view the beauty of Red Rock Canyon; the road is located just off SR 159 and open daily from 7 a.m. to dusk. This one-way, 13-mile route begins near the visitor center, then returns to SR 159 about two miles farther south. The drive offers a close look at the area's Aztec sandstone, plant life and the **Keystone Thrust Fault**. The fault occurred some 65 million years ago and is considered the most significant geologic feature of Red Rock Canyon. It is believed that two of the Earth's crustal plates collided with such force that part of one plate was shoved up and over the younger sandstone. The thrust contact is evidenced by the sharp contrast between the gray limestone and the red sandstone.

The first two pullouts on the scenic loop have short trails to the base of the **Calico Hills**, where seasonal rain pools can be found. These pools often become temporary homes to small insects, insect larvae and fairy shrimp. Easier hiking can be found a little farther along the drive at the **Sandstone Quarry** (a short, graded dirt road leads to this spot). From the historic quarry, many small canyons can be explored. A side road leads to the Willow Spring Picnic Area and a ³⁄₁₀-mile hike from the road takes visitors to **Lost Creek Canyon**, the site of a year-round spring and occasional seasonal waterfall.

Farther along the gently curving drive is **Ice Box Canyon Overlook**. From this location, visitors can take a ⅝-mile hike to a box canyon surrounded by steep walls; the walls keep this canyon cooler than others in the area—hence the name. The end of the hike is reached by "boulder hopping" an additional ½ mile across the canyon bottom. Seasonal pools and an occasional waterfall can also be found here. The last stop along the road is the **Pine Creek Canyon Overlook**, one of the area's most popular hiking trails. The two-mile round trip features a running creek, ponderosa pines and the remains of a historic homestead.

The scenic loop drive is also an excellent way for experienced **bicyclists** to see the area. The one-way paved road assures riders of no oncoming traffic, and since the road is two lanes wide, there is plenty of room for cars to pass. Bicyclists will, however, find the road a

*The Scenic Loop Drive offers views of the vivid red sandstone in the Calico Hills.*

bit of a challenge. Its steep, undulating grades gain 1000 feet in altitude over the first five miles, followed by switchbacks at the top of the grade, then by a 1000-foot drop in elevation over the last eight miles. Round-trip mileage is about 15 miles. Bicyclists should beware of weekend and holiday traffic, which can be heavy, and keep a lookout for falling rocks in the switchbacks and loose pebbles and debris where the road crosses a wash. Since there is no repair facility or air for tires available in the park or in nearby Blue Diamond, cyclists should come prepared to make their own repairs. The visitor center has a brochure detailing the route.

**Safety Guidelines:**

- Thunderstorms, especially in summer and early fall, can produce both lightning and flash floods. Never drive across flooded roads or cross low-lying areas when water is running.
- Charcoal fires are allowed at designated sites where grills are provided. Ground fires are prohibited.
- Camping is permitted only in designated locations.
- Climbing on sandstone requires equipment and experience. Sandstone is soft and crumbly and can be dangerous to climbers.
- Heat, cold and dehydration can take their toll on hikers. Carry one gallon of water for each person per day. Summer days can bring extreme heat, and temperatures drop rapidly at night.
- All natural and historic features are protected by federal law. This includes animals, plants, rocks and American Indian artifacts. Do not damage, disturb or remove them.
- Do not feed the burros at Red Rock Canyon. Feeding burros encourages them to congregate on the roads, where many have been killed or injured by vehicles. Burros have also been known to bite, kick and step out in front of cars unexpectedly. Use caution and observe them from a distance.

**BONNIE SPRINGS OLD NEVADA** *Off SR 159/W. Charleston Blvd., 5½ miles south of the Red Rock Canyon Visitor Center; 1 Gun Fighter Ln., 89004. (702) 875-4191. Open daily; during daylight-saving time 10:30 a.m.-6 p.m., standard time to 5 p.m.; tickets sold until one hour before closing. Petting zoo open daily; during daylight-saving time 10 a.m.-6 p.m., standard time to 5 p.m. Train operates Sat., Sun. and holidays only. Admission to Old Nevada: adults, $6.50; ages 62 and over, $5.50; ages 5-11, $4; train rides and petting zoo, free.* In the 1800s Bonnie Springs Ranch was a stopover for wagon trains traveling the Old Spanish Trail. In 1952, Al and Bonnie Levinson built a replica of an old western town here and fashioned it into a tourist attraction. Free activities include the petting zoo and rides on a miniature train. The petting zoo has donkeys, pigs, llamas, deer, a variety of other farm animals and a duck pond; food to feed them can be purchased from on-site vending machines. For a fee, visitors can experience the Old Nevada Village, a western-style town that offers staged gunfights and hangings, a melodrama, wax museum, blacksmith display, stagecoach rides, horseback rides and more. A western-themed motel, gift shop, restaurant and saloon are also on the premises.

**SPRING MOUNTAIN RANCH STATE PARK** *South of Scenic Loop Dr., off SR 159; P.O. Box 124, Blue Diamond 89004. (702) 875-4141; summer theater information (702) 594-7529. Day-use area open 8 a.m. to dusk.* **Visitor center/ranch house** *open Mon.-Fri. noon-4 p.m., Sat., Sun. and* *holidays 10 a.m.-4 p.m. Guided tours of the historic area Fri.-Mon. and holidays; call for schedule. Entrance fee, $5 per vehicle.* This 528-acre park at the base of the majestic Wilson Cliffs overflows with tranquil beauty. Listed on the National Register of Historic Sites, the area was once the alternate route of the Old Spanish Trail during the 1830s, a welcome oasis for weary travelers. Through most of this century the site was used as a cattle ranch, changing ownership several times (including with Howard Hughes), before coming under park protection in 1974. Tours of the historic site and its circa 1860s structures are given throughout the year. A large, grassy day-use area, shaded by scrub oak and mesquite trees, is available for picnickers; tables and barbecue grills are provided. The park hosts many activities, including summer musicals, at its outdoor theater June through August, and living history programs in the spring and fall.

# Spring Mountains National Recreation Area

*35 miles northwest of Las Vegas via US 95, turnoff at SR 157/Kyle Canyon Rd. or SR 156/Lee Canyon Rd.* **Visitor Center (Las Vegas)** *located 4 blocks west of Sahara Blvd. at 2881 S. Valley View Blvd., Ste. 16, 89102. (702) 873-8800. Open Mon.-Fri. 8 a.m.-4:30 p.m. Closed Sat., Sun. and holidays.* **Visitor center (Kyle Canyon)** *located at Mile Marker 3 on SR 157. (702) 872-5486. Hours vary; call for information.* Barely a 45-minute drive from the glitz of Las Vegas is Spring Mountains National Recreation Area. Part of the Humboldt-Toiyabe National Forest, Spring Mountains NRA provides a lush reprieve from high temperatures and stark landscapes of the desert. By taking the Spring Mountains Scenic Loop, visitors are exposed to a number of appealing sights as the road climbs to

*Joshua trees line the entrance to Spring Mountain Ranch State Park.*

*Spring Mountains National Recreation Area offers snow sports in the winter and a lush reprieve from high desert temperatures in the summer.*

its maximum elevation of 8500 feet. At this elevation, the temperature in the forest is usually 30 degrees cooler than in Las Vegas. Weekend crowds attest to the forest's popularity; weekdays are usually quieter.

*Caution:* Portions of the national forest may close for the winter as early as October (depending on weather conditions), and tire chains may be required at any time during winter months. Gasoline is not available on the mountain.

**Cathedral Rock**, **Old Mill**, **Foxtail** and **Deer Creek** are enjoyable picnic spots. Another feature to look for is **Mummy Mountain**, so named because it looks like a huge mummy lying on its back. Restaurant dining with outdoor seating is available near Cathedral Rock. Hikers should bring comfortable walking shoes in order to experience the area's beauty close-up; numerous hiking trails offer broad vistas and interesting flora and fauna.

**Charleston Peak** is the third highest peak in Nevada. A trail to the 11,918-foot summit is usually open between June and October, though weather conditions can lengthen or shorten the hiking season considerably. Hikers should be in good condition before attempting the climb; the gain in elevation from start to finish is almost 4000 feet, and the total round trip is more than 18 miles.

**LAS VEGAS SKI AND SNOW-BOARD RESORT** *47 miles northwest of Las Vegas via US 95 and SR 156/Lee Canyon Rd. (702) 385-2754. Open Thanksgiving to Easter, daily 9 a.m.-4 p.m.* Rentals (alpine skis, boots and poles, snowboards), snowmaking, night skiing, ski school, snack bar and

day lodge are all available. Runs are 15 percent novice, 65 percent intermediate and 20 percent advanced, with the longest run being ⅗ mile. The vertical drop is 1000 feet. Three double chairs service the area; prices vary, call for information. The nearest AAA-approved accommodations are in Las Vegas. Remember that tire chains may be required when driving to this area.

# Valley of Fire State Park

*50 miles northeast of Las Vegas via I-15 and SR 169 (Valley of Fire Rd.); P.O. Box 515, Overton 89040. (702) 397-2088. Entrance fee: $4 per vehicle. Camping fee: $11 per vehicle.* **Visitor center** *located just off Valley of Fire Rd. midway into the park. Open daily 8:30 a.m.-4:30 p.m. Closed Jan. 1 and Dec. 25.* So named because of the effect of bright sunlight reflecting off red sandstone, Valley of Fire State Park is a visually stunning area that contains dozens of unique geological formations and remnants of an ancient American Indian civilization.

During the dinosaur age 150 million years ago, these great sandstone formations were created from shifting sand dunes and years of uplifting, faulting and erosion. Prehistoric inhabitants of the area included the Basket Maker people, and later, the Anasazi Pueblo farmers from the nearby Moapa Valley.

There are literally countless natural formations here, brilliantly red in color, and all different shapes and sizes. **Elephant Rock** is one of the most photographed, located near the east entrance station; it looks like the profile of an elephant when viewed from the hill behind, looking toward Valley of

Fire Road. **Seven Sisters** is another striking formation, and easily visible from Valley of Fire Road, just east of the visitor center. **The Beehives**, weathered by wind and water, are near the west entrance station. The remnants of petrified logs are also within in the park, although thoughtless visitors have taken so many samples that the amount of petrified wood is considerably depleted.

*Elephant Rock is one of the most photographed formations in Valley of Fire State Park.*

For examples of **petroglyphs**—pictures carved into rock—**Atlatl Rock** is one of the best. Situated near the center of the park along Scenic Loop Road, the petroglyphs of the towering rock are easily viewed by walking up a steep, metal staircase. Visitors who brave the 83 mesh-covered steps to the top will be rewarded with the sight of ancient, well-preserved figures carved into the rock. Another site known for its petroglyphs is **Mouse's Tank**, a natural basin named after an early renegade who used the area as a hideout. Water collects in the rock after a rainfall, occasionally remaining in the tank for months.

Because of its rare beauty, Valley of Fire has been used many times as the background for motion pictures. There are numerous hiking trails, as well as camping and picnicking facilities. The visitor center has an outdoor botanical garden, displays of local fauna, and information about the park and its hiking trails.

*A climb to Atlatl Rock is richly rewarded with close-up views of Indian petroglyphs.*

*Caution:* Care should be taken when traveling in this area.

- Thunderstorms, especially in summer and early fall, can produce both lightning and flash floods. Camp only in designated areas and never drive across flooded roads.

- All natural and historic features are protected. This includes animals, plants, rocks and American Indian artifacts. Do not damage, disturb or remove them.

- Care should be taken when hiking in canyon areas. Taking shortcuts may be dangerous. Never hike alone. Register at the visitor center before hiking backcountry areas. No overnight backpacking.

## GUIDED TOURS

The tours listed in this section generally last less than a day, though some of the trips to more distant places involve an overnight stay. Be sure to contact the companies in advance for complete information and reservations, including deposit requirements and cancellation notice; scheduled tours are subject to cancellation if there is an insufficient number of passengers. Many tours offer hotel pickup and discounted children's rates.

*Tours listed are provided as a convenience for our readers; inclusion in this publication does not imply endorsement by the Automobile Club of Southern California.*

## Boulder City

**BLACK CANYON RAFT TOURS**
*1297 Nevada Hwy., 89005. (800) 696-7238, (702) 293-3776. Feb. through*
*Nov. Closed Dec. and Jan. Adults, $64.95; ages 5-12, $35. Lunch included. Reservations advised.* Colorado River raft trips from Hoover Dam to Willow Beach.

**GRAND CANYON AIR SAFARIS**
*1301 Airport Rd.; P.O. Box 60035, 89006. (702) 293-1848, 293-9906; FAX (702) 294-0232.* Grand Canyon, Hoover Dam/Lake Mead air and air/land packages.

**LAKE MEAD CRUISES** *P.O. Box 62465, 89006. (702) 293-6180. Midday sightseeing cruise: adults, $16; ages 2-11, $6. Evening dinner/dance cruise (Fri. and Sat. only): adults, $43. Early dinner cruise (Sun-Thu.): adults, $29; ages 2-11, $15. Breakfast cruise (Sat. and Sun. only): adults, $21; ages 2-11, $10. Reservations recommended.* Lake Mead sternwheeler boat cruises departing from Lake Mead Marina with stops at Hoover Dam.

## SHOWROOM ENTERTAINMENT

### Primm

Located along I-15 at the California and Nevada state lines, this emerging area offers production shows, special events and lounge entertainment. Times and prices vary with entertainers.

**BUFFALO BILL'S RESORT AND CASINO**
*On east side of I-15. (702) 386-7867, (800) 386-7867.*

**Star of the Desert Arena** — Top-name entertainment and special events.

## PRIMADONNA RESORT AND CASINO
*On east side of I-15. (702) 386-7867, (800) 386-7867.*

**Primadonna Showroom** — Top-name entertainment.

## WHISKEY PETE'S HOTEL AND CASINO
*On west side of I-15. (702) 386-7867, (800) 386-7867.*

**Whiskey Pete's Showroom** — Top-name entertainment.

## ANNUAL EVENTS

The Boulder City area plays host to a number of annual events, while Logandale, more than 50 miles northeast of Las Vegas, hosts the Clark County Fair each year. For detailed information about each event, please call the telephone numbers shown or consult with the local chamber of commerce or visitor information bureau.

### April

**CLARK COUNTY FAIR** *Clark County Fairgrounds, Logandale, Nev. (702) 398-3247.* This four-day event features livestock shows, American Indian dancing, pony rides, arts and crafts booths and carnival rides.

### May

**SPRING JAMBOREE & CRAFT FAIR** *Bicentennial Park, Boulder City, Nev. (702) 293-2034.* A two-day arts and crafts fair, classic car show, food booths and music are all part of this springtime festival.

### July

**DAMBOREE** *Boulder City, Nev. (702) 293-2034.* Fourth of July events include a parade, games, children's activities, live music, a carnival and fireworks.

### September

**RATTLIN' RAILS HANDCAR RACES** *Boulder City, Nev. (702) 293-4857.* Four-person teams from as far away as Canada compete in different categories over two days, racing handcars down a pair of railroad tracks. A barbecue and awards ceremony follow.

### October

**ART IN THE PARK** *Bicentennial Park, Boulder City, Nev. (702) 294-1611.* With arts and crafts on display in more than 300 booths, this two-day show is the largest of its kind in the western United States.

### December

**CHRISTMAS PARADE** *Boulder City, Nev. (702) 293-2034.* A Saturday morning parade down the Nevada Highway, ending at Bicentennial Park, helps celebrate the holiday season.

**PARADE OF LIGHTS** *Lake Mead. (702) 293-2034 (Boulder City, Nev.).* Boats ranging in size from 16 to 34-plus feet long gather on the nation's largest manmade lake to ring in the Christmas season with an evening's blaze of festive, twinkling lights.

# Laughlin-Bullhead City

*Ninety miles south of Las Vegas are the booming towns of **Laughlin, Nev.,** and **Bullhead City, Ariz.** Perched on opposite banks of the Colorado River, they lack the thrill rides or go-go atmosphere of Las Vegas, but have won a large following in their own right. Laughlin alone draws nearly 5 million tourists annually, wooed by a relaxed pace, and bargain-priced lodging and meals at its riverside hotel-casinos. Seniors especially have taken to the town, where big band music and singers of decades past are major draws on the lounge and showroom circuit. Some 10,000 to 15,000 "snowbirds" migrate from colder climes each year to make the area their winter home.*

*Moreover, the region boasts many worthwhile attractions, ranging from hiking trails and Davis Dam to an antique car collection and several historic mining towns. And of course, there's abundant recreation on the Colorado River.*

## POINTS OF INTEREST

Attractions are listed alphabetically. Note: the State of Arizona does not observe daylight-saving time. Mountain Standard Time is in effect year round.

### COLORADO RIVER MUSEUM
*On the Arizona side of the river on SR 95, ½ mile north of the Laughlin Bridge; P.O. Box 1599, Bullhead City 86430. (520) 754-3399. Open 9 a.m.-2:30 p.m. (Arizona time); Nov. through Mar. daily; Apr. through Oct. Tue.-Sat. Closed Jul., Aug., Jan. 1, Thanksgiving, Dec. 25. Donation.* Housed in a former Catholic church built in 1947 during the Davis Dam construction, this small museum features a model of Fort Mohave in the late 1800s, geologic maps of the area and historical photographs. Items donated to the museum include a steamboat anchor, mining tools, antique barbed wire, American Indian artifacts and a piano that was shipped around Cape Horn 130 years ago.

### DAVIS CAMP COUNTY PARK *On the Arizona side of the river on SR 95, ½ mile north of the Laughlin Bridge; P.O. Box 2078, Bullhead City 86430. (520)* 754-4606. *Open daily, 24 hours; day use ends at 8 p.m. $3 entrance fee; $5 holiday weekends.* The park offers a stretch of sandy beach for swimming and fishing or launching personal watercraft, inner tubes, rafts or rubber boats. The area from the park north to Davis Dam is noted for its excellent striped bass and rainbow trout fishing. Visitors have found that a hike into the park's south section can provide views of a variety of birds and small wildlife. Camping is permitted in an RV park and along the river (see *Campgrounds & Trailer Parks*); fishing requires a license (see Water Recreation under *Recreation*).

### DAVIS DAM *2 miles north of Laughlin via Casino Dr. and SR 163; U.S. Bureau of Reclamation, Davis Dam, Bullhead City 86429. (520) 754-3628.* The dam, designed to help regulate the delivery of water to the lower Colorado River region and Mexico, is a rock-fill and earthen structure augmented by concrete intakes and spillways. In addition to its importance for flood control, the dam provides hydroelectric power for regional industry and irrigation for farming. The powerhouse is no longer open for tours, but the dam can still be viewed up close.

*Several Laughlin hotels boast their own boat docks.*

**DON LAUGHLIN'S CLASSIC CAR COL- LECTION** *Don Laughlin's Riverside Resort Hotel & Casino, 1650 S. Casino Dr., Laughlin; P.O. Box 500, 89029. (702) 298-2535, ext. 5678 or 5103. Open daily; Mon.-Fri. 9 a.m.-10 p.m., Sat. and Sun. hours extend- ed to 11 p.m. Free.* The col- lection features antique, classic and futuristic "concept" automobiles from the Imperial Palace in Las Vegas and Don Laughlin's private collection. The cars are exhibited in two rooms: a glass- walled room facing Casino Drive and the Exhibition Hall on the third floor of the hotel's new 28-story tower.

**GAMBLING TRAIN OF LAUGH- LIN** *Ramada Express Hotel & Casino, 2121 South Casino Dr.; P.O. Box 77771,* 89028. *Open daily; Sun-Thu. 11 a.m.-7 p.m., Fri.-Sat. 10 a.m.-10 p.m. Free.* This narrow-gauge train offers rides (but no gambling) around the parking lot of this railroad-themed hotel. The locomotive is a replica of the Genoa, an 1890s-era steam engine that hauled freight and passengers on the Virginia and Truckee line in western Nevada. Adjacent is the Great Train Store, a gift and souvenir shop for railroad enthusiasts.

*Davis Dam spans the Colorado River near Laughlin.*

LAUGHLIN-
LAKE HAVASU REGION

FREEWAY & ACCESS RAMPS
PAVED ROAD
UNPAVED ROAD
POINT OF INTEREST
GOLF COURSE
AAA APPROVED HOTEL OR MOTEL
CAMPGROUND
BOATING FACILITY
MISCELLANEOUS RECREATION

SCALE IN MILES

0     5     10

MAP 2776

# ▼ A Quick Guide to Laughlin-Bullhead City

## Population
| | |
|---|---|
| Bullhead City | 28,535 |
| Laughlin | 8,500 |

## Elevation
| | |
|---|---|
| Bullhead City | 540 ft. |
| Laughlin | 510 ft. |

## Emergency          911

## Highway Conditions
| | |
|---|---|
| Arizona | (520) 779-2711 |
| Nevada | (702) 486-3116 |

## Time/Weather
| | |
|---|---|
| Arizona | (520) 763-3000 |
| Nevada | time (702) 844-1212 |
| | weather (702) 248-4800 |

## Emergency Road Service for AAA Members
(800) AAA-HELP (in the USA and Canada)
(800) 955-4TDD (for the hearing impaired)

## Newspapers
The Laughlin-Bullhead City area's daily newspaper is the *Mohave Valley Daily News and Booster/Advertiser*. The major weeklies are the *Bullhead City Bee*, the *Weekender* and the *Laughlin Nevada Times*. Another publication of note is the *Laughlin Entertainer*, which provides news on lounge and showroom acts in the community.

## Radio Stations
Classic Rock: KLUK (108 FM); Contemporary Rock: KZUL (95.3 FM), KZZZ (100.3 FM); Country: KFLG (102.7 FM and 1000 AM), KGMN (104.7 FM), KWAZ (97.9 FM); News/Talk: KQAAA (1230 AM); Oldies: KRCY (105.9 FM).

## TV Stations
In Laughlin, the major television stations include channels 3 (NBC), 5 (FOX), 8 (ABC) and 13 (CBS). In Bullhead City, Ariz., the major network programs appear on channels 5 (CBS), 10 (FOX), 12 (NBC) and 13 (ABC). For a complete list of television programs, consult the daily newspaper or hotel listings.

## Public Transportation
### Shuttles and Ferries
All of the hotels in Laughlin have large on-site parking lots. A **water taxi** runs between the casino docks at the Riverside, Edgewater, Pioneer, Golden Nugget and Harrah's; the fare is $2 one way and $3 round trip. On those occasions when the water level of the river (controlled by Davis Dam) is too low for the taxis to travel safely, parking lot pickups are made by shuttle buses.

In addition, Citizen Area Transit (CAT) operates a 24-hour **bus route** in Laughlin, covering the business district and residential area. The fare for those 18 and over is $1.50, and 75¢ for ages 65 and older and 5 to 17.

## Taxi

Laughlin and Bullhead City both have taxi service, but the Arizona-based taxi companies are not allowed to operate in Nevada unless called to take a passenger from Laughlin into the state of Arizona; they are not allowed to take passengers from one casino to another or from one location in Nevada to another.

The Laughlin taxi company charges a base fare of $2.20 plus $1.50 for each mile; 30¢ per minute waiting time. Rates are unregulated for cabs operating in Bullhead City, so fares vary by company.

### Laughlin

| | |
|---|---|
| Desert | (702) 298-7575 |
| Lucky | (702) 298-2299 |

### Bullhead City

| | |
|---|---|
| Bullhead City Taxi | (520) 754-7433 |
| Checker | (520) 754-4444 |
| Lucky | (520) 754-1100 |
| Tri-State | (520) 758-1024 |

## Hospitals

Bullhead Community Hospital
2735 Silver Creek Rd.
Bullhead City, AZ 86442
(520) 763-2273

Mohave Valley Hospital and Medical Center
1225 Hancock Rd.

Bullhead City, AZ 86442
(520) 758-3931

Laughlin Medical Center
150 E. Edison Way
Laughlin, NV 89029
(702) 298-3364

## AAA/California State Automobile Association

Henderson District Office
601 Whitney Ranch Dr., #A
Henderson, NV 89014
(702) 458-2323
Office hours: Mon.-Fri. 8:30 a.m.-5 p.m.

Las Vegas District Office
3312 W. Charleston Blvd.
Las Vegas, NV 89102
(702) 870-9171
Office hours: Mon.-Fri. 8:30 a.m.-5 p.m.

## Visitor Services

Bullhead Area Chamber of Commerce
1251 Hwy. 95
Bullhead City, AZ 86429
(520) 754-4121
Office hours: Mon.-Fri. 9 a.m-5 p.m., Sat. 10 a.m.-2 p.m.

Laughlin Visitors Bureau
1555 Casino Dr.
P.O. Box 29849
Laughlin, NV 89029
(702) 298-3321, (800) 452-8445
Office hours: Open daily 8 a.m.-5 p.m.

**GRAPEVINE CANYON/
CHRISTMAS TREE PASS** *7 miles
west of Davis Dam on SR 163 (about 6
miles west of Casino Dr.), north on dirt
access road (a small sign indicates the
turn).* (520) 754-3272. This canyon
offers excellent viewing of American
Indian rock carvings of animals, fertili-
ty symbols and spiritual signs. These
petroglyphs, which vary in age from
150 to more than 600 years old, are
reached by a half-mile path from the
parking area. Hikers will travel along
the edge of a wash to a small incline
in the canyon. Rangers lead hikes into
the canyon twice weekly (except
during summer). Primitive restrooms
are available at the parking lot and
hikers must bring their own drinking
water.

Heading north from the Grapevine
Canyon parking lot (toward US 95)
leads to Christmas Tree Pass, which
gets its name from the piñon and
juniper trees that locals have decorated
with ribbons, plastic lids, paper and
other bits of "trash" for many years.
About four miles out of Grapevine

Canyon the wide, graded dirt road nar-
rows considerably to allow access for
only one car in each direction; this
section is not recommended for RVs.
As the road leaves Christmas Tree Pass
it widens out again for another five
miles to US 95. **Note:** This road is
subject to heavy washout during periods of rain.

**Four-wheel-drive** enthusiasts will find
several backcountry roads that the
National Park Service has approved for
public access. They lead to secluded
coves on the lake or into the desert
mountain backcountry. It is advisable
to check with the ranger for information about road conditions. *Caution:*
Flash flooding can occur during
inclement weather and sudden summer
thunderstorms. Watch for unfenced
mine shafts and pits. Stay out of abandoned mines; deep shafts, rotten timbers, and flammable or poisonous gases
can be concealed inside the tunnels.

**HORIZON OUTLET CENTER**
*Corner of Casino Drive and Edison
Way, at 1955 S. Casino Dr, Laughlin,*

*Historic Route 66 offers spectacular mountain scenery near Oatman.*

*Among Oatman's residents are wild burros that regularly roam the streets.*

*Nev., 89029. (702) 298-3003. Open daily; Mon.-Sat. 10 a.m.-9 p.m., Sun to 6 p.m.* This 225,000-square-foot indoor mall has more than 50 factory outlet stores, a food court and a movie theater. The complex features Art Deco design throughout.

**OATMAN** *23 miles southeast of Bullhead City, Ariz. via SR 95 and Boundary Cone Rd., on historic Route 66 (Oatman Hwy.). (520) 768-8070.* Located in the rugged Black Mountains between Kingman and Bullhead City on historic Route 66, Oatman is an old mining town that is still brimming with the fervor of the Old West. Many of the original buildings are still in use, housing tourist-oriented enterprises, as well as a post office and several western-style restaurants and saloons.

A prosperous gold-mining community from 1906 to 1942, local mines yielded nearly $36 million in gold at the peak of production. It was the onset of World War II that led to the town's demise, when Congress halted all mining not essential to the war effort.

Today Oatman has about 150 residents, down from a whopping 10,000 during its heyday in the 1930s. Oatman's fortuitous position along the original Route 66 (US 66) from Chicago to Los Angeles has undoubtedly helped preserve it; this town was an important last stop for travelers before entering the Mojave Desert into California.

A number of wild west-style attractions can be seen here, including the **staged gunfights** most Saturdays, Sundays and holidays; the Oatman Jail; the historic Oatman Hotel (where movie legends Clark Gable and Carole Lombard spent their wedding night in 1939); and the town's unofficial reception committee of **wild burros.** These cute, dusty animals are descendants of the burros miners turned loose years ago. They freely roam the streets in search of carrot handouts, a snack that can be purchased in local stores.

For an interesting **scenic drive** take historic Route 66 (Oatman Highway) northeast out of Oatman to Kingman. The road goes past the abandoned mining camp of **Goldroad,** climbs to the summit of the Black Mountains, then crosses the wide Sacramento Valley to **Kingman.** At times the road becomes a series of narrow hairpin curves as it winds its way up to the pass. But those with an adventurous spirit will be rewarded with panoramic views of Arizona and Nevada (maybe even California on a clear day) from the tri-state lookout point just before the summit of Sitgreaves Pass. From here, descend the eastern slope of the Black Mountains into the Sacramento Valley, an area populated with creosote bushes, yucca plants and, in season, a sprinkling of wildflowers. For the return to the Laughlin Bridge, take SR 68 west from Kingman across the flat Sacramento Valley, through a pass at the north end of the Black Mountains and down into the Colorado River Valley back to the bridge. Total mileage (from Oatman) is 60 miles. **Note:** This trip is not recommended for large RVs or trailers.

*Caution:* When exploring near these areas, a four-wheel-drive vehicle is recommended for travel on unpaved roads. Flash flooding can occur during summer thunderstorms, and heavy rains are possible in any season. When exploring old gold camps, watch out for unfenced mine shafts and pits. Never enter abandoned mines; deep shafts, rotted timbers and flammable or poisonous gases can be concealed in the tunnels.

## GUIDED TOURS

The tours listed in this section generally last less than a day, though some of the trips to more distant places involve an overnight stay. Be sure to contact the companies in advance for complete information and reservations; many tours offer hotel pickup and discounted children's rates. Scheduled tours are subject to cancellation if there is an insufficient number of passengers.

*Tours listed are provided as a convenience for our readers; inclusion in this publication does not imply an endorsement by the Automobile Club of Southern California.*

**BLUE RIVER SAFARIS** *Mailing address: P.O. Box 31998, 89028. (702) 298-0910, (800) 345-8990. Departures from Colorado Belle, Edgewater, Flamingo Hilton or Riverside Resort hotels. Tickets sold on board boats or buses.* Lake Havasu City/London Bridge, Oatman, Hoover Dam, Grand Canyon boat and land tours.

***DEL RIO YACHT*** *Harrah's Casino Hotel, 2900 W. Casino Dr., 89029. (800) 742-3224. Departures from Harrah's Casino Hotel boat dock. Tickets available at dock.* Laughlin-Bullhead City area, Davis Dam boat tours.

**LAUGHLIN RIVER TOURS, INC.** *P.O. Box 29279, 89028. (702) 298-1047, (800) 228-9825. Depending on* *cruise, departures at Gold River, Flamingo Hilton or Edgewater boat docks. Tickets available at docks of all three hotels.* Laughlin-Bullhead City area tours aboard paddle-wheel boat.

**U.S.S. RIVERSIDE** *Don Laughlin's Riverside Resort Hotel & Casino, 1650 S. Casino Dr., 89029. (702) 298-2535, ext. 5770, (800) 227-3849, ext. 5770. Departures from Don Laughlin's Riverside boat dock. Ticket booth located on the ground level of hotel, next to boat dock.* Laughlin-Bullhead City area, Davis Dam boat tours.

## SHOWROOM ENTERTAINMENT

Laughlin does not offer the elaborate, long-running stage shows for which Las Vegas is famous. But its showrooms, cabarets and lounges do offer a variety of entertainment ranging from headline performers to lounge acts. While the facilities listed here seat 500 or more, many smaller venues are popular as well. Showroom listing does not imply AAA endorsement for the lodging establishment. For the most current information, refer to the Auto Club's "Las Vegas Shows" schedule, available to AAA members at all district offices.

Lounge entertainment is available at all of the casinos, although some do not offer shows on Monday. The Riverside's Western Ballroom on the second floor of the hotel's south tower features a tea dance every Sunday from 2 to 6 p.m.; reservations are not needed. In the evenings, the ballroom features live country music and dancing on its 1400-square-foot dance floor. Also, the Ramada Express offers dance con-

tests Tuesday through Saturday at 4 p.m. in the Caboose Lounge. Times and prices vary with entertainers.

### DON LAUGHLIN'S RIVERSIDE RESORT HOTEL & CASINO
*1650 S. Casino Dr. (702) 298-2535, ext. 616, (800) 227-3849.*

**Don's Celebrity Theatre** — *Reservations not required.* Top-name entertainment.

### FLAMINGO HILTON-LAUGHLIN
*1900 S. Casino Dr. (702) 298-5111, (800) 435-8469.*

**Amphitheatre** — *Outdoor seating in spring and fall.* Top-name entertainment.

**Club Flamingo** — Top-name entertainment.

### GOLD RIVER GAMBLING HALL AND CASINO
*2700 S. Casino Dr. (702) 298-2242, (800) 835-7904.*

**Cody's Saloon** — Top-name entertainment.

### HARRAH'S CASINO HOTEL
*2900 W. Casino Dr. (702) 298-7111, (800) 237-1739.*

**Fiesta Showroom** — Top-name entertainment.

### RAMADA EXPRESS HOTEL & CASINO
*2121 S. Casino Dr. (702) 298-4200, (800) 243-6846.*

**Pavilion Showroom** – Top-name entertainment.

## ANNUAL EVENTS

Car and motorcycle rallies, rodeos, and fireworks displays, even a sidewalk egg fry, are among the many annual community events that Laughlin and environs have to offer. For detailed information about each event, please call the telephone numbers shown or consult with the local chamber of commerce or visitor information bureau.

In addition, casino tournaments take place in many Laughlin area casinos. Anyone interested in these tournaments should contact the hotel or venue directly for dates and play information; room reservations should be made well in advance, as room space is often at a premium during a tournament.

### January

**DOWNHILL BED RACES** *Oatman, Ariz. (520) 768-6222.* During mid-January, five-person teams push old iron beds to the finish line on a downhill, zigzag race course.

**LAUGHLIN DESERT CHALLENGE** *Starts and finishes at corner of Big Bend Drive and Edison Way, Laughlin, Nev. (800) 227-5245 or (702) 298-2214.* More than 200 of the world's top drivers compete over two days in an off-road race through the rough terrain outside of Laughlin.

**TURQUOISE CIRCUIT FINALS RODEO** *Corner of Marina Blvd. and Hwy. 95, Bullhead City, Ariz. (520) 754-4121.* This professional Cowboy Association-sanctioned event features three days of calf-roping, bareback bull and bronco riding, music, food and vendor booths.

### March

**SILVERY COLORADO RIVER ROCK CLUB GEMBOREE** *Bullhead City Jr. High School, Bullhead City, Ariz. (520) 758-3099. Some years takes place in Apr.* This two-day event features displays of rocks, including rocks for purchase, and demonstrations of lapidary, silversmithing and faceting.

### April

**DESERT TWIRLERS JAMBOREE** *Mohave High School, Bullhead City, Ariz. (520) 768-1794, 763-3424.* This two-day event features square and round dancing, plus daytime workshops.

**LAUGHLIN RIVER RUN** *Casino Dr., Laughlin, Nev. (800) 227-5245 or (702) 298-2214.* This four-day motorcycle rally features Harley Davidsons and is billed as the West Coast's largest motorcycle event. Vendor booths sport a wide range of merchandise, such as motorcycle accessories, silver and turquoise jewelry and leather apparel. Live entertainment and food are also featured.

**RODEO DAYS** *Casino Dr., Laughlin, Nev. (800) 227-5245, (702) 298-2214.* Hundreds of participants compete for prize money in eight traditional rodeo events. Entertainment, vendor booths and Southwestern-style fun at area resorts are also part of the celebration.

### May

**RIVER DAYS** *Colorado Riverfront, Laughlin, Nev. (800) 227-5245 or (702) 298-2214.* Amateur and professional riders compete over three days in personal watercraft races on the

Colorado River along the Laughlin shoreline. An exposition showcases the latest in personal watercraft equipment and accessories.

## July

### FOURTH OF JULY FESTIVITIES
*Various locations. (702) 298-2214 (Laughlin, Nev.), (520) 754-4121 (Bullhead City, Ariz.), (520) 768-8070 (Oatman, Ariz.).* Independence Day is celebrated in a wide range of community events.

### OATMAN SIDEWALK EGG FRY
*Oatman, Ariz. (520) 768-8070.* This annual Fourth of July event features an egg and spoon race, traditional sidewalk egg fry, egg toss and chicken leg contest.

## September

### CORN FEST *Mohave Valley, Ariz. (520) 768-2777.* Eating contests, including corn and pies, and live entertainment are part of this three-day festival.

### OATMAN GOLD CAMP DAYS
*Oatman, Ariz. (520) 768-6222.* The internationally famous Burro Biscuit Throwing Contest is the highlight of this Labor Day weekend event. Other activities include a crazy hat contest, chili cookoff and barbecue.

### RODDIN' ON THE RIVER *Don Laughlin's Riverside Resort Hotel & Casino, Laughlin, Nev. (520) 754-*

*5112.* Hot rods, classic customs and mini trucks are showcased during this four-day event. Highlights include slow drags and valve-cover races.

## October

### LAUGHLIN RIVERFLIGHT
*Corner of Big Bend Dr. and Edison Wy., Laughlin, Nev. (702) 298-2214.* Balloon pilots participate in this three-day race and rally over the Mohave Desert and Colorado River. Food booths, an arts and crafts fair, chili cookoff and outdoor concert are also featured.

## December

### CHRISTMAS BUSH FESTIVAL
*Oatman, Ariz. (520)-768-6222.* Shopkeepers and residents spend a day decorating bushes for the holidays along historic Route 66 leading into Oatman from the west.

### PARADE OF LIGHTS *Katherine Landing, Ariz. (520) 754-3245.* Boats gather on Lake Mohave to celebrate the Christmas season with an evening's blaze of festive, twinkling lights.

### NEW YEAR'S EVE CELEBRATIONS *(702) 298-2214 (Laughlin, Nev.), (520) 754-4121 (Bullhead City, Ariz.).* Traditional New Year's Eve festivities take place on both sides of the Colorado River.

# Recreation

*With an average of nearly 300 sunny days a year, **Las Vegas** and the **Laughlin-Bullhead City** area are ideal spots for outdoor sports. Not only are there acres of lush green golf courses, tennis courts and seemingly endless swimming pools, but the canyons and mountains offer horseback riding amid dramatic backdrops, and the **Lake Mead National Recreation Area** provides year-round boating, fishing, water-skiing and more.*

## Golfing

Golf is one of the principal outdoor attractions in Las Vegas, as well as a popular sport in Laughlin-Bullhead City. Las Vegas features several championship courses, some of which host PGA and LPGA tournaments, plus several less demanding courses where the weekend golfer can enjoy a quick round. The desert climate offers nearly ideal playing conditions all year, with the exception of very high midday temperatures in July and August. In summer, golfers should arrange an early starting time to avoid the extreme heat.

Public, semi-private and private courses are listed alphabetically by city. Information given for each course includes its name, location, street address, phone number, yardage, par, slope, USGA ratings (from the preferred tee of the course), greens fees and facilities. Greens fees are given for weekday and weekend play during peak season. Some courses may not allow walking so the greens fee includes the *mandatory* golf cart fee. Some courses have senior citizen rates; call for information. Information not available or not applicable is indicated by the abbreviation **N/A**. Unless otherwise stated, each course is open daily.

Military golf courses listed in this publication show greens fees that apply to civilian guests of military personnel. Nine-hole courses may show par, slope and USGA rating that reflect nine holes played twice with two separate tees, or *two tees*. It follows that many 9-hole courses may list 18-hole fees because they require 18 holes of play.

All semi-private and private courses have restrictions on public play ranging from members and guests only to liberal reciprocal agreements with members of other courses. Information on private courses is not listed, but a telephone number is provided for obtaining information about reciprocal play. As it is impossible to list all of the restrictions for each course, telephoning the course is highly recommended in lieu of knowing a member. Reservations are advised at most courses; some country clubs require reservations months in advance.

Information in this section is published as it is received from the individual courses. The listings have been made as complete as possible.

### Boulder City

**BOULDER CITY GOLF COURSE**
Public
*Southeast of US 93 off Buchanan Blvd.; 1 Clubhouse Dr., 89005. (702) 293-9236. Daily rate: $27.* The course is 18 holes; 6132 yards; par 72; 103 slope; 68.3 rating. Clubhouse, golf shop, professional, power carts, rental clubs, driving range; coffee shop, snack bar.

### Henderson

**BLACK MOUNTAIN GOLF AND COUNTRY CLUB** Semi-Private
*½ mile southwest of US 93 (Boulder Hwy.); 500 Greenway Rd., 89015. (702) 565-*

7933. *Closed Dec. 25. Rates: Mon.-Fri. $50, Sat.-Sun. (including golf cart) $55.* The course is 18 holes; 6541 yards; par 72; 120 slope; 69.1 rating. Clubhouse, locker room, golf shop, professional, power carts, rental clubs, driving range; restaurant, coffee shop, snack bar.

## THE LEGACY GOLF CLUB Public
*North of SR 146 (Lake Mead Dr.) off N. Green Valley Pkwy.; 130 Par Excellence Dr., 89014. (702) 897-2187. Closed Dec. 25. Rate including mandatory golf cart: Mon.-Thu. $115, Fri.-Sun. $125.* The course is 18 holes; 6211 yards; par 72; 118 slope; 69.1 rating. Clubhouse, golf shop, professional, power carts, rental clubs, driving range; restaurant, snack bar.

## WILDHORSE GOLF CLUB Public
*3 miles west of US 95 via Sunset Rd. and Green Valley Pkwy.; 1 Showboat Country Club Dr., 89014. (702) 434-9009. Rates including mandatory golf cart: Mon.-Thu. $70-110, Fri.-Sun. $85-135.* The course is 18 holes; 5954 yards; par 72; 124 slope; 69.7 rating. Golf shop, professional, power carts, rental clubs, driving range; restaurant, snack bar.

## Las Vegas

## ANGEL PARK GOLF CLUB Public
*5 miles west of SR 95 off Summerlin Pkwy.; 100 S. Rampart Blvd., 89128. (702) 254-4653. Closed Dec. 25. Daily rate including mandatory golf cart: $110.* The **Mountain Course** is 18 holes; 5751 yards; par 71; 116 slope; 67.8 rating. The **Palm Course** is 18 holes; 5857 yards; par 70; 120 slope; 69.8 rating. Clubhouse, locker room, golf shop, professional, power carts, rental clubs, driving range,

night lighting for courses and driving range; restaurant, snack bar.

## BADLANDS GOLF CLUB Public
*3½ miles west of US 95 via Summerlin Pkwy. off Rampart Blvd.; 9115 Alta Dr., 89128. (702) 242-4653. Daily rate including mandatory golf cart: $98-115.* The course is 18 holes; 6500 yards; par 72; 113 slope; 67.8 rating. Clubhouse, golf shop, professional, power carts, rental clubs, driving range; restaurant, coffee shop, snack bar.

*Golf is a popular pastime at Las Vegas' numerous courses.*

## CANYON GATE COUNTRY CLUB
Private
*(702) 363-0303.*

## CRAIG RANCH GOLF COURSE
Public
*3 miles north off I-15/US 93; 628 W. Craig Rd., 89030. (702) 642-9700. Daily rate: $14.* The course is 18 holes; 6001 yards; par 70; 105 slope; 66.8 rating. Clubhouse, golf shop, professional, power carts, rental clubs, driving range; snack bar.

## DESERT INN GOLF CLUB
Semi-Private
*¾ mile east of I-15 off Flamingo Rd.; 3145 Las Vegas Blvd. S., 89109. (702) 733-4290. Daily nonhotel guest rates*

*including mandatory golf cart: $195.*
The course is 18 holes; 6270 yards; par
72; 118 slope; 69.8 rating. Clubhouse,
locker room, golf shop, professional,
power carts, rental clubs, driving range;
tennis, swimming; restaurant, coffee
shop, snack bar.

## DESERT PINES GOLF CLUB
Public
*Just north of US 95 via Eastern Ave.;*
*3415 E. Bonanza Rd., 89101. (702)*
*388-4400. Rates including mandatory*
*golf cart: Mon.-Thu. $115, Fri.-Sun.*
*$130.* The course is 18 holes; 6810
yards; par 71; 112 slope; 66.8 rating.
Clubhouse, golf shop, professional,
power carts, rental clubs, driving range,
night lighting for driving range; restaurant, snack bar.

## DESERT ROSE GOLF COURSE
Public
*6 miles east of I-15 off Sahara Ave.;*
*5483 Clubhouse Dr., 89122. (702) 431-*
*4653. Daily rate: $48.50.* The course is
18 holes; 6511 yards; par 71; 119 slope;
69.6 rating. Clubhouse, golf shop,
professional, power carts, rental clubs,
driving range; restaurant, snack bar.

## HIGHLAND FALLS GOLF
## COURSE Semi-Private
*10 miles northwest of downtown off Lake*
*Mead Blvd.; 10201 Sun City Blvd.,*
*89134. (702) 363-4373. Daily rate*
*including mandatory golf cart: $53-95.*
The course is 18 holes; 6512 yards; par
72; 126 slope; 71.2 rating. Clubhouse,
golf shop, professional, power carts,
rental clubs, driving range, night lighting for driving range; coffee shop,
restaurant, snack bar.

## LAS VEGAS COUNTRY CLUB
Private
*(702) 734-1122.*

## LAS VEGAS GOLF CLUB Public
*1½ miles north of US 95 via Decatur*
*Blvd.; 4300 Washington Ave., 89107.*
*(702) 646-3003. Daily rate: $16.75.*
The course is 18 holes; 6337 yards; par
72; 114 slope; 70.3 rating. Golf shop,
professional, power carts, rental clubs,
driving range, night lighting; snack bar.

## LAS VEGAS HILTON COUNTRY
## CLUB Public
*3 miles east of I-15 via Flamingo Rd.*
*and Maryland Pkwy.; 1911 E. Desert*
*Inn Rd., 89109. (702) 734-1062. Rates*
*including mandatory golf cart: Mon.-*
*Thu. $108-120, Fri.-Sun. $135-150.* The
course is 18 holes; 6418 yards; par 71;
121 slope; 70.2 rating. Clubhouse,
locker room, golf shop, professional,
power carts, rental clubs, driving range,
night lighting for driving range; restaurant, snack bar.

## LAS VEGAS PAIUTE RESORT
Public
*18 miles northwest of downtown off US*
*95 at Exit 95 (Snow Mountain), 1½*
*miles east to 10325 Nu-Wav Kaiv Blvd.,*
*89124. (702) 658-1400. Two courses;*
*rates for both including mandatory golf*
*cart: Mon.-Thu. $100, Fri.-Sun. $110.*
The **Snow Mountain Course** is 18
holes; 6035 yards; par 72; 112 slope;
68.6 rating. The **Sun Mountain
Course** is 18 holes; 6074 yards; par 72;
116 slope; 68.6 rating. Clubhouse, golf
shop, professional, power carts, rental
clubs, driving range; restaurant, coffee
shop, snack bar.

## LOS PRADOS GOLF COURSE
Public
*8 miles northwest of US 95 via Lone*
*Mountain Rd. and Los Prados Blvd.;*
*5150 Los Prados Cir., 89130. (702) 645-*
*5696. Closed Dec. 25. Rates: Mon.-Fri.*
*$40, Sat.-Sun. and holidays $45.* The
course is 18 holes; 4937 yards; par 70;

107 slope; 65.8 rating. Clubhouse, locker room, golf shop, professional, power carts, rental clubs; restaurant, coffee shop, snack bar.

## NORTH LAS VEGAS COMMUNITY 3 PAR GOLF COURSE Public
*1 mile west of I-15 off Cheyenne Ave.; 324 E. Brooks Ave., 89036. (702) 633-1833. Rates: Mon.-Fri. $5-6.50, Sat.-Sun. and holidays $6.50-7.50.* The course is 9 holes; 1128 yards; par 27; N/A slope; N/A rating. Clubhouse, rental clubs, driving range, night lighting; coffee shop, snack bar.

## PAINTED DESERT GOLF COURSE Public
*¼ mile west of US 95 (Tonopah Hwy.) off Ann Rd.; 5555 Painted Mirage Wy., 89129. (702) 645-2568. Rates including mandatory golf cart: Mon.-Thu. $53-99, Fri.-Sun. $70-130.* The course is 18 holes; 6323 yards; par 72; 128 slope; 71.0 rating. Clubhouse, golf shop, professional, power carts, rental clubs, driving range; restaurant, snack bar.

## PALM VALLEY GOLF CLUB
Semi-Private
*10 miles northwest of downtown off Lake Mead Blvd.; 9201-B Del Webb Blvd., 89128. (702) 363-4373. Daily rate including mandatory golf cart: $95.* The course is 18 holes; 6800 yards; par 72; 127 slope; 72.3 rating. Clubhouse, golf shop, professional, power carts, rental clubs, driving range; restaurant, snack bar.

## SUNRISE COUNTRY CLUB
Semi-Private
*(702) 456-3160.*

## SUNRISE VISTA GOLF COURSE
Private
*(702) 652-2602.*

## TOURNAMENT PLAYERS CLUB AT SUMMERLIN Private
*(702) 256-0111.*

## TOURNAMENT PLAYERS CLUB AT THE CANYONS Public
*4 miles west of US 95 off Summerlin Pkwy., Town Center and Village Center drs. at 9851 Banburry Cross Rd. (702) 256-2000. Rates including mandatory golf cart: Mon.-Thu. $115, Fri.-Sun. $130.* The course is 18 holes; 6110 yards; par 71; 118 slope; 67.7 rating. Clubhouse, locker room, golf shop, professional, power carts, rental clubs, driving range; restaurant, snack bar.

# Laughlin-Bullhead City

## CHAPARRAL COUNTRY CLUB
Public
*7 miles south of Laughlin Bridge via SR 95; 1260 Mohave Dr., Bullhead City, AZ 86442. (520) 758-6330, 758-3939. Closed Dec. 25. Daily 18-hole rate: $25.* The course is 9 holes; 2306 yards; par 32; 100 slope; 62.1 rating. Clubhouse, golf shop, professional, power carts, rental clubs; snack bar.

## DESERT LAKES GOLF CLUB
Public
*13 miles south of Laughlin Bridge via SR 95, east on Joy Ln.; 5835 Desert Lakes Dr., Bullhead City, AZ 86430. (520) 768-1000. Winter rates including mandatory golf cart: Mon.-Thu. $57.75, Fri.-Sun. $66.15; call for summer, senior and twilight rates.* The course is 18 holes; 6569 yards; par 72; 119 slope; 70.5 rating. Clubhouse, golf shop, professional, power carts, rental clubs, driving range; coffee shop.

## EMERALD RIVER GOLF COURSE Public
*1½ miles east of Needles Hwy.; 1155 S.*

*Casino Dr., Laughlin, NV 89029. (702) 298-0061. Rates including mandatory golf cart: Mon.-Thu. $50, Fri.-Sun. $60.* The course is 18 holes; 5918 yards; par 72; 131 slope; 69.1 rating. Clubhouse, golf shop, professional, power carts, rental clubs, driving range; snack bar.

**RIVERVIEW GOLF COURSE**
Public
*5 miles south of Laughlin Bridge via SR 95, east to 2000 E. Ramar Rd., Bullhead City, AZ 86442. (520) 763-1818. Winter rates: Mon.-Fri. $12 (9 holes) and $18 (18 holes); Sat.-Sun. $15 (9 holes) and $20 (18 holes). Call for summer rates.* The course is 9 holes; 1160 yards; par 27; N/A rating. Clubhouse, golf shop, professional, hand carts, power carts, rental clubs.

## Primm

**PRIMM VALLEY GOLF CLUB**
Semi-Private
*(800) 386-7867.*

## Spring Mountains National Recreation Area

**MOUNT CHARLESTON GOLF RESORT** Public
*30 miles northwest of Las Vegas on SR 157, near Mount Charleston Hotel; 1 Kyle Canyon Rd., Las Vegas, 89124. (702) 872-4553. Daily rate including mandatory golf cart: $55 for 9 holes, $75 for 18 holes.* The course is 9 holes; 3106 yards; par 70 (9 holes twice); N/A rating. Golf shop, professional, power carts, rental clubs, driving range; snack bar.

# Horseback Riding

## Boulder City

**2R RIDING STABLES AT HOOVER DAM** *US 93, 1 mile west of*

*Hoover Dam; P.O. Box 62266, 89006. (702) 293-3434 (stables), (702) 256-7433 (office). Open daily 8 a.m.-dusk. $20 per person. Reservations recommended.* One-hour narrated rides provide panoramic views of Hoover Dam, Lake Mead and Black Canyon. Custom outings to other locales available.

## Las Vegas

**COWBOY TRAIL RIDES, INC.**
*1211 S. Eastern Ave., 89124. (702) 387-2457. Open daily. Guided rides ranging from 1 hour to overnight; prices from $20 to $225, depending on length of ride. Reservations recommended.* Riders traverse scenic Red Rock Canyon on trips varying widely in length. Custom outings to Mt. Charleston, Lee Canyon, Lovell Canyon and Valley of Fire State Park also available.

## Red Rock Canyon National Conservation Area

**BONNIE SPRINGS OLD NEVADA** *Off SR 159/W. Charleston Blvd., 5½ miles south of Red Rock Canyon Visitor Center; 1 Gun Fighter Ln., 89004. (702) 875-4191. Open daily; first ride departs at 9 a.m., last at 3:15 p.m., Jun. through Sep. at 5:45 p.m. $18 per person. No reservations.* One-hour guided rides traverse scenic Red Rock Canyon.

## Spring Mountains National Recreation Area

**MOUNTAIN T RANCH** *140 Kyle Canyon Rd., Las Vegas, NV 89124. (702) 656-8025. Open daily. 1½, 2½, 3½ hours to all-day guided rides; prices range from $20 to $100, depending on length of ride. Reservations accepted; no credit cards. Lunch and barbecue outings available.* Starting from an elevation of

*Outdoor activities include horsing around with a new friend at Red Rock Canyon.*

4300 feet, guided rides ascend to the 5000- to 6000-foot level, covering the La Madre Mountain Range and the high desert just below Mount Charleston.

# Rock Climbing

## Red Rock Canyon National Conservation Area

**SKY'S THE LIMIT** *HCR 33 Box 1, 89124. (702) 363-4533, (800) 733-7597. Half-day rock climbing lessons $169. Reservations recommended.* Participants learn climbing and rappelling fundamentals from experienced instructors amid the scenery of Red Rock Canyon. Climbing shoes and equipment are provided. Day hikes also available.

# Tennis & Racquetball

Tennis and racquetball enthusiasts will find plenty of places to hone their skills in Las Vegas. A number of publicly maintained parks have courts, as do many of the resort hotels and private clubs. Most of the courts are lighted for nighttime play. The hotels that allow visitors to use their facilities often give priority to their registered guests, restricting others to open courts. Hotels whose courts are for guests only are not listed here. It is always a good idea to phone ahead, since hours and regulations governing play are subject to change.

The public courts operate on a first-come, first-served basis, and are open daily, generally from 6 a.m. to 11 p.m. Call the Sunset Park Community Center at (702) 455-8245 for reservations or more information about public courts.

## Las Vegas

**BALLY'S LAS VEGAS** Semi-Private *3645 Las Vegas Blvd. S., 89109. (702) 739-4598. Hotel guests, $8 per hour; nonguests, $15 per hour. Reservations required for play between 7 a.m. and 7 p.m.* 8 lighted outdoor tennis courts.

**DESERT INN** Semi-Private *3145 Las Vegas Blvd. S., 89109. (702) 733-4577. Hotel guests, free; nonguests, $10 daily pass. Reservations available.* 4 lighted tennis courts.

**FLAMINGO HILTON-LAS VEGAS** Semi-Private *3555 Las Vegas Blvd. S., 89109. (702) 733-3444. $12 per hour for hotel guests, $20 for nonguests.* 4 lighted tennis courts.

**HIDDEN PALMS PARK** Public *8855 Hidden Palms Parkway, 89123.* 2 lighted tennis courts.

### LAS VEGAS ATHLETIC CLUB-MARYLAND PARKWAY
Semi-Private
*2655 S. Maryland Pkwy. (702) 734-5822. Open 24 hours. Guest pass, $10. Reservations available.* 5 racquetball courts.

### LAS VEGAS ATHLETIC CLUB-SPRING MOUNTAIN ROAD
**AT I-15** Semi-Private
*3315 Spring Mountain Rd., 89102. (702) 362-3720. Open daily; Mon.-Fri. 5 a.m-11 p.m., Sat. and Sun. 8 a.m.-8 p.m. Guest pass: $10. Reservations available.* 8 racquetball courts.

### LAS VEGAS SPORTING HOUSE
Semi-Private
*3025 Industrial Rd., 89109. (702) 733-8999. Open 24 hours. $15 per person, includes all facilities.* 10 racquetball courts; 2 squash courts; 2 lighted tennis courts.

### LAURELWOOD PARK Public
*4300 Newcastle Rd., 89103.* 2 lighted tennis courts.

### MGM GRAND HOTEL CASINO
Semi-Private
*3799 Las Vegas Blvd. S., 89109. (702) 891-3085. Hotel guests $15, nonguests $20. Reservations advised.* 4 lighted tennis courts. Racquet rentals, lessons, ball machine.

### MONTE CARLO RESORT & CASINO Semi-Private
*3770 Las Vegas Blvd. S., 89109. (702) 730-7411. Hotel guests $10, nonguests $15. Reservations required.* 3 lighted tennis courts.

### PARADISE PARK COMMUNITY CENTER Public
*4770 S. Harrison Dr., 89121.* 2 lighted tennis courts.

### PAUL MEYER PARK Public
*4525 New Forest Dr., 89117.* 2 lighted tennis courts.

*The desert climate offers nearly ideal playing conditions year round.*

2240 Linn Ln., 89115.

EGAS Semi-Private

SUNRISE PARK AND
COMMUNITY CENTER** Public
*2240 Linn Ln., 89115.* 2 lighted tennis
courts.

**SUNSET PARK** Public
*2575 E. Sunset Rd., 89120. $5 per person
per hour. Reservations required.* 8 lighted
tennis courts. Frisbee golf course.

**UNIVERSITY OF NEVADA,
LAS VEGAS** Semi-Private
*McDermott Complex, on campus, near
Harmon Ave. and Swenson St. Tennis
reservations (702) 895-4489; racquetball
reservations (702) 895-3150. Tennis
courts open daily 8 a.m.-10 p.m. Guest
fee $5. Racquetball courts open daily;
Mon.-Fri. 6 a.m.-10 p.m., Sat. 8 a.m.-6
p.m., Sun. 10 a.m.-6 p.m. Guest fee, $2.
Reservations advised.* 12 lighted tennis
courts; 8 indoor racquetball courts.

**WHITNEY PARK AND
COMMUNITY CENTER** Public
*5700 E. Missouri Ave., 89122.* 3 lighted
tennis courts.

**WINCHESTER PARK AND
COMMUNITY CENTER** Public
*3130 S. McLeod Dr., 89121.* 2 lighted
tennis courts.

**WINTERWOOD PARK** Public
*5310 Consul Ave., 89122.* 2 lighted
tennis courts.

## Laughlin

**MOUNTAIN VIEW PARK** Public
*Needles Hwy., south of Desert Rd.* 2
lighted tennis courts.

# Water Recreation

Entries for this section are listed north
to south in three regions along the
Colorado River: Lake Mead, Lake

Mohave and Below Davis Dam. The
first two fall within the Lake Mead
National Recreation Area, which
stretches from the upper reaches of
Lake Mead to Davis Dam at the southern tip of Lake Mohave. The river
below Davis Dam includes the
Laughlin/Bullhead City area and
southward toward Needles, Calif.

## Lake Mead

*25 miles southeast of Las Vegas; 4 miles
northeast of Boulder City. Information
available through the Lake Mead
National Recreation Area at either the*

## ▼ Spa Facilities

After a long day of exploring the
diverse offerings of Las Vegas, your
tired and aching muscles may be
screaming out for a relaxing massage, facial or herbal wrap. On the
other hand, maybe your body is
used to a regular workout and you
feel guilty about lounging around
the hotel pool or casino all day, or
worse, the number of buffets
you've been frequenting. Alas, help
is on the way! Many of the large
resort hotels feature complete spa
facilities, including whirlpool,
sauna, massage, exercise programs
(aquatic, aerobic), gym equipment,
and more. Hotel spa and health
club privileges often carry a fee;
policies vary at each establishment.
Some health clubs in hotels admit
only registered guests. Public
health clubs are numerous in the
city, and most of the larger ones
offer daily passes; check the local
telephone directory yellow pages
under "Health Clubs" for further
information.

**Alan Bible Visitor Center** *on US 93, phone (702) 293-8990 or 293-8906, or at any park ranger station.* Elevation 1200. This 110-mile-long lake on the Colorado River extends from Hoover Dam to the Grand Canyon. The shoreline offers sandy beaches and sheltered coves, while the rugged desert terrain invites hiking and climbing. Lake activities encompass boating, swimming, sailing, water-skiing, scuba diving, sailboarding, use of personal watercraft and fishing. Complete recreation facilities are available at six sites operated by concessionaires of the National Park Service. Boaters should beware of sudden winds, floating debris, and underwater rocks and shoals caused by fluctuating water levels.

*Lake Mead National Recreation Area features a variety of water sports.*

## Boating

**Callville Bay Resort and Marina** *22 miles northeast of Henderson on SR 167, 4 miles south of Northshore Rd.; Box 100, HCR 30, Las Vegas, NV 89124. (702) 565-8958. Open daily.* Paved launch ramp, temporary mooring, slips, dry storage, auto/boat fuel, engine repairs, marine waste station. Rentals: houseboats, motorboats (15 to 130 h.p.), fishing tackle, jet skis, houseboats. Marine hardware, campground, picnic area.

**Echo Bay Resort and Marina** *30 miles south of Overton off Northshore Rd., Overton, NV 89040. (702) 394-4066. Open daily.* Paved launch ramp, temporary mooring, slips, dry storage, auto/boat fuel, engine and hull repairs, marine waste station. Rentals: houseboats, motorboats (15 to 150 h.p.), fishing tackle, water-skis, personal watercraft. Marine hardware, bait, groceries, ice, snack bar, restaurant, lodging, campground, picnic area.

**Hemenway Launch Ramp** *5 miles northeast of Boulder City off Lakeshore Rd.; Lake Mead National Recreation Area, 601 Nevada Hwy., Boulder City, NV 89005. (702) 293-8990. Open daily.* Paved launch ramp. Wheelchair-accessible fishing dock nearby.

**Lake Mead Resort and Marina** *7 miles northeast of Boulder City; 322 Lakeshore Rd., Boulder City, NV 89005. (702) 293-3484. Open daily.* Paved launch ramp, slips, temporary mooring, dry storage, boat fuel. Rentals: motorboats (140 h.p.). Lodging, public campgrounds, restaurant, store; picnic area nearby.

**Las Vegas Bay Marina** *8 miles northeast of Henderson off Lakeshore Rd.; P.O. Box 91150, Henderson, NV 89009. (702) 565-9111. Open daily.* Paved launch ramp, temporary mooring, slips, dry storage, auto/boat fuel, engine and hull repairs, marine waste station. Rentals: motorboats (15 to 185 h.p.), water-skis. Marine hardware, bait, groceries, ice, restaurant, campground, picnic area.

**Overton Beach Resort and Marina**
*11 miles southeast of Overton off Lakeshore Rd., Overton, NV 89040. (702) 394-4040. Open daily. Closed Dec. 25.* Paved launch ramp, temporary mooring, slips, dry storage, auto/boat fuel, engine and hull repairs, marine waste station. Rentals: personal watercraft. Marine hardware, bait, groceries, ice, snack bar, RV sites with hookups.

**Temple Bar Resort and Marina** *28 miles northeast of US 93 at end of Temple Bar Rd.; P.O. Box 545, Temple Bar, AZ 86443. (520) 767-3211. Open daily. Closed Dec. 25.* Paved launch ramp (fee), mooring, slips, dry storage, auto/boat fuel, engine/hull repairs, marine waste station. Rentals: motorboats (15 to 150 h.p.), fishing tackle, water-skis, personal watercraft. Marine hardware, bait, groceries, ice, restaurant, lodging, public campground, picnic area.

## Fishing

Lake Mead offers some of the country's best fishing. Unlike some lakes, Lake Mead (and nearby Lake Mohave) has an open season on all species of fish year round. Largemouth bass, striped bass, channel catfish, black crappie and bluegill are popular catches; rangers or marina personnel can help point out the best fishing areas. Striped bass are most popular; some have tipped the scales at 50 pounds or more. A wheelchair-accessible fishing dock is located at Hemenway Fishing Point on Boulder Beach.

## Swimming

Clear and clean water ideal for swimming, snorkeling and diving can be found at Lake Mead. The best seasons are spring, summer and fall, when water temperatures average about 78 degrees. Boulder Beach is a designated swimming area. Swim with caution and with a buddy, as no lifeguard services are provided. The scuba diving trail at north Boulder Beach provides a protected dive area.

## ▼ *Houseboating*

Houseboats are permitted on Lake Mead, Lake Mohave and on the 75-mile stretch of the Colorado River from Davis Dam south to Parker Dam. There are 246 square miles of uncrowded, open waters for houseboaters on Lake Mead. The numerous secluded coves and scenic steep-walled canyons along its 550 miles of shoreline make the area popular with boaters. The Colorado River section from Davis Dam south offers varied scenery, including rugged mountains, marshes, a narrow canyon (south of Needles) and the wide expanse of Lake Havasu. Lake Mohave has numerous coves and inlets to explore at the south end of the lake, including many sandy coves. The mild winter weather and hot summer days make houseboating popular all year in each of these areas; however, summer thunderstorms are common. Reservations should be made well in advance. Houseboats can be rented at the following locations: **Lake Mead:** Callville Bay Resort and Marina, (800) 255-5561; Echo Bay Resort, (800) 752-9669. **Lake Mohave:** Cottonwood Cove Resort and Marina, (800) 255-5561; Lake Mohave Resort, (800) 752-9669.

# Water-Skiing

The lake's wide basins offer perfect conditions for water-skiing. The sport is allowed on most of Lake Mead, except in the side canyons and north of Hoover Dam for a few hundred feet.

## Lake Mohave

*Accessible via US 95 and US 93. Information available through the Lake Mead National Recreation Area at either the* **Alan Bible Visitor Center** *(near Lake Mead on US 93), phone (702) 293-8990 or 293-8906, or at any park ranger station.* Elevation 675. This narrow lake, which stretches for 67 miles below Hoover Dam to Davis Dam, is lined by rock canyon walls and has numerous coves and sandy beaches. Activities include boating, swimming, water-skiing, skin diving, sailboarding, use of personal watercraft and fishing. Boating facilities are located at three points along the lake. Boaters should beware of sudden winds and flash floods.

## Boating

**Cottonwood Cove Resort and Marina** *14 miles east of Searchlight at end of Cottonwood Cove Rd.; P.O. Box 1000, Cottonwood Cove, NV 89046. (702) 297-1464. Open daily.* Paved launch ramp, slips, dry storage, auto/boat fuel, engine repairs, temporary mooring, marine waste station. Rentals: Houseboats, motorboats (15 to 130 h.p.), personal watercraft, water-skis. Bait, groceries, ice, clothing, restaurant, lodging, RV sites with hookups, picnic and swimming areas.

**Lake Mohave Resort and Marina** *At Katherine Landing, 6 miles north of Bullhead City via Arizona SR 68 and Katherine Landing Rd., Bullhead City, AZ, 86430. (520) 754-3245. Open daily.* Paved launch ramp, slips, temporary mooring, dry storage, boat fuel, engine repairs, marine waste station. Rentals: houseboats, motorboats (15 to 150 h.p.), fishing tackle, water-skis, personal watercraft, houseboats. Marine hardware, bait, groceries, ice, snack bar, restaurant, lodging, RV sites with hookups, picnic area. Wheelchair-accessible fishing dock nearby.

**Princess Cove Launch Ramp** *Follow a graded dirt road 3 miles north of Katherine Landing, Bullhead City; Lake Mead National Recreation Area, 601 Nevada Hwy., Boulder City, NV 89005. (702) 293-8990.* Paved launch ramp.

**Willow Beach Harbor** *14 miles south of Hoover Dam via US 93 and Willow Beach Rd.; Willow Beach, AZ 86445. (520) 767-4747. Open daily. Closed Dec. 25.* Paved launch ramp, slips, auto/boat fuel, marine waste station. Rentals: motorboats (25 h.p.). Bait, groceries, ice, picnic area.

## ▼ *More on the River*

Visitors will find the Auto Club's *Guide to Colorado River* to be a useful recreation map of the Colorado River. The guide provides detailed map coverage and information on local activities, attractions, events and facilities. Members can obtain this publication at all Auto Club district offices in California and Nevada. Nonmembers should check with a local bookseller in Central or Southern California.

## Fishing

Noted for its rainbow trout and bass fishing, Lake Mohave offers an open season on all species of fish year round. Trout spend the summer north of Willow Beach and migrate south from October through January; a fish hatchery at Willow Beach provides trout for planting in the lake. Rainbow trout are popular in the cold waters of upper Lake Mohave from Hoover Dam to Willow Beach, but the record sizes of the past have diminished to an occasional five pounds. Large-mouth bass prefer the deep water at the south end of the lake and only move into shallow water to spawn; the best catches are taken from October to May. Trolling live bait at depths of 10 to 30 feet works well to lure them; fishing the coves with floating minnow-shaped lures is also effective during the midday hours. Striped bass have become an increasingly common catch through much of the lake in recent years. July and August are the best months for finding catfish in the lake's small coves and inlets. February through April is crappie season; they can be found along the lower half of the lake. Mini-jigs, worms and minnows are the ticket for catching them. A wheelchair-accessible fishing dock is located at Katherine Landing. **Note:** There is a multiagency effort under way to protect endangered species of the Colorado River. Fishermen should identify and immediately release humpback chubs, bonytail chubs, razorback suckers and Colorado squawfish that they hook. Anglers who are unfamiliar with these species will find descriptions in the California and Arizona fishing regulations booklets that are available where licenses are sold.

## Swimming

Lake Mohave offers swimming, snorkeling and diving in clear waters. Except for the northern reaches of the lake, where the water is quite cold, the water averages about 78 degrees during spring, summer and fall.

## Water-Skiing

Water-skiing is permitted on all of Lake Mohave except along a 21-mile stretch of the Colorado River extending south from Hoover Dam to Chalk Cliffs.

## Colorado River: Below Davis Dam

*Accessible via Arizona SR 95.* Elevation 550. This stretch of the Colorado River is bordered by mobile home parks and the many casinos of Laughlin, Nevada. Activities include swimming, water-skiing, sailboarding, use of personal watercraft and fishing. Supplies and tourist facilities are available in Bullhead City and Laughlin, and boat launching ramps are scattered along the shoreline.

## Boating

**Bullhead City Rotary Park** *2315 Balboa Dr.; P.O. Box 21179, Bullhead City, AZ 86439. (520) 763-9400 ext. 138. Open daily.* Paved launch ramp ($7.50 entry fee in summer). Picnic area.

**Davis Camp County Park** *Mohave County Park; P.O. Box 2078, Bullhead City, AZ 86430. (520) 754-4606. Open daily.* Paved launch ramp ($3 entry fee), dry storage. Ice, tent and RV sites, picnic area.

**Lazy Harry's** *Off Riverview Dr; 2170 Rio Grande Rd, Bullhead City, AZ*

86442. *(520) 758-6322. Open daily. Paved launch ramp. Ice, restaurant, picnic area.*

# Fishing

Rainbow trout are the most popular catch along this stretch of the river; they inhabit the cold water along the gravel beds below Davis Dam (no fishing in posted areas). Trout are also planted south of Laughlin-Bullhead City near the California-Nevada state line from October to June. During warm weather, the fish are attracted to

---

## ▼ *Fishing Licenses*

Anglers fishing from Arizona, California and Nevada must possess valid fishing licenses from the state concerned. In Arizona, persons under age 14 do not require a license, while in California persons under age 16 do not require one. In Nevada a junior permit is required for anglers 12 to 15 years old. The rules and regulations of each state must be strictly adhered to, including within the Lake Mead National Recreation Area. Fishing on the Colorado River or Lake Mead requires a "special use" stamp affixed to a state fishing license. An additional stamp is required for trout fishing. Fishing from shore on an Indian Reservation requires a special fishing permit. Licenses and further information are available from the marinas or at local bait and tackle shops.

---

lures such as Super Dupers, Panther Martins, and spinners and spoons. (No, we're not making this up.) In cooler weather, the best bet is live bait, mostly night crawlers and marshmallow combos. The fish stay in deep water during the day and move toward shore at night.

Anglers can also fill their creels with good-sized catfish, largemouth bass, and plenty of bluegill and crappie. Bass prefer the cooler deep water and will hit on live bait or floating lures. Catfish like stink baits (garlic-cheese), dough balls, anchovies and night crawlers. Bluegill and crappie hit on almost anything that moves—try worms for bluegill, and minnows or mini-jigs for crappie.

Striped bass are a popular game fish, and they often tip the scales around 30 pounds. The largest striper ever caught in an inland habitat was landed at Bullhead City and weighed in at 59 pounds, 12 ounces. These fish winter at Lake Havasu and start moving north in the spring, hitting the Laughlin-Bullhead City area in May; common baits are shad, frozen anchovies or sardines, with sinkers to keep the bait below the surface of the water. The **Striper Derby** is traditionally held from Memorial Day through Labor Day. Call the Bullhead Area Chamber of Commerce at (520) 754-4121 for the current status of the event.

## LAUGHLIN SPORTFISHING
*Harrah's Casino Hotel boat dock, 2900 W. Casino Dr., Laughlin; P.O. Box 29010, 89029. (702) 298-6828. Open daily, weather permitting; boat departs at 6 a.m. $50 per person. Reservations required.* Half-day boat excursions provide trout and striped bass fishing

*The beach at Harrah's Laughlin is a pleasant spot for taking a dip and enjoying the sight of passing riverboats.*

opportunities on the Colorado River. All bait and tackle supplied.

## Inner Tubing

Inner tubing is a popular sport along the Colorado River. For easy pickup and parking, swimmers usually launch their inner tubes from Davis Camp County Park, north of Bullhead City, Arizona, float four or five miles south along the river and disembark at Bullhead Community Park.

## Swimming

Swimming in the river should not be attempted except from designated beach areas. A public beach is located at Davis Camp County Park on the Arizona side of the river (north of Bullhead City on SR 95). **Note:** A word of caution to river swimmers south of Davis Dam—the water released from the dam is very cold, about 60 degrees. The best swimming in the area is at Lake Mohave. In the summer the lake water can get as warm as 80 degrees.

## Water-Skiing

Water-skiing is allowed along the Colorado River from Bullhead City south to Needles. A sparsely populated area just south of Bullhead City is usually the best choice for the sport.

# Transportation

*A rich variety of transportation choices to **Las Vegas** and **Laughlin** make getting there a breeze. Both desert cities boast international airports, convenient bus service and well-maintained roads.*

## Air

For complete schedule information and help arranging flights from cities with direct or connecting service, contact any **Auto Club Travel Agency** office, or phone the Auto Club's Airline Express Desk. In Southern California call (800) 222-5000, Monday through Friday from 8 a.m. to 6 p.m.; in Northern California call (800) 352-1955, Monday through Friday 8 a.m. to 5:30 p.m.

### LAUGHLIN/BULLHEAD INTERNATIONAL AIRPORT

*600 Hwy. 95, Bullhead City, AZ 86429. (520) 754-2134.* This $23 million airport is located in Arizona just minutes from the casino gaming action across the river. The 7500-foot-by-150-foot runway accommodates aircraft as large as DC-10s, and is served by two commuter airlines and three charter carriers. About 100 flights are logged each week, serving more than 230,000 passengers a year. Taxis and free hotel shuttles serve the airport, and several car rental agencies have offices here.

### McCARRAN INTERNATIONAL AIRPORT

*1 mile from the Las Vegas Strip; 5757 Wayne Newton Blvd., Las Vegas 89119. (702) 261-5211; TDD (702) 261-3111 for the hearing impaired.* McCarran is the 10th busiest airport in the U.S. and 15th busiest in the world, with more than 30 million passengers passing through it each year. More than 40 air carriers serve Las Vegas, among them 21 scheduled airlines, two commuter lines and up to 20 charter airlines (depending on the season), including two weekly nonstops from Europe. The facility averages some 800 flights a day.

Passenger traffic has exploded in recent years, rising 200 percent since 1985. The airport has responded with a $500 million expansion project scheduled for completion in the fall of 1998. The centerpiece of the expansion will be a new concourse adding 26 new gates for aircraft. Long-term plans call for the airport to have some 135 gates by the year 2010, compared to the 1997 total of 67.

Shuttle buses, taxis, limousines and buses make pickups at McCarran every half hour. The Citizens Area Transit (CAT) number "108" and "109" buses serve the airport; call (702) 228-7433 for further details. Ground transportation services at McCarran are abun-

*McCarran International Airport serves more than 30 million passengers annually.*

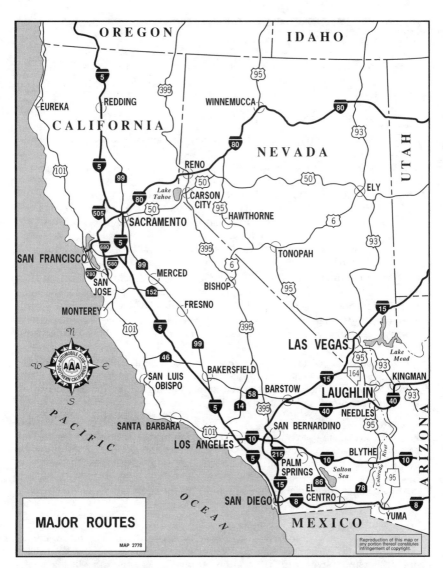

**MAJOR ROUTES**

MAP 2778

dant, see the Las Vegas telephone directory yellow pages under "Airport Transportation & Parking Services." All major car rental companies have offices at McCarran; refer to the yellow pages under "Automobile Renting and Leasing." The Auto Club's Travel Agency offices and Airline Express Desk can also help arrange reservations for a car rental.

# Automobile

**Las Vegas** entertains millions of visitors each year, and not surprisingly more than half of them arrive by automobile. More than 4 million people a year drive to Nevada's largest city from the state of California. Southern Californians account for most of the automobile traffic. With the 70 mph speed limit in

# ▼ *Desert Driving Hints*

Regardless of the point of departure, any automobile trip from California to Las Vegas will involve some desert driving. At all times, but especially during the summer months, some basic precautions should be taken when planning to cross the Mojave Desert.

- Check the condition of your car's engine and cooling systems and make sure they're in good working order. Look closely for radiator leaks, worn fan belts and cracked hoses.
- Take about five gallons of water in a clean container for emergency purposes—both for the car's radiator and for drinking. If your car overheats, do not remove the radiator cap immediately because of the risk of explosion. After the engine has cooled, slowly remove the cap and add water, leaving about an inch of air space between the water level and the top of the radiator. If an older model car experiences vapor lock, wrap a wet towel around the gas line between the fuel pump and the carburetor. This should cool the line and allow the car to start.
- Make certain that your car's tires are properly inflated before starting out. If the tires become overly hard while crossing the desert, do not release any air. Instead, stop the car and allow the tires to cool, then proceed.
- Watch the gasoline gauge and buy fuel when it is available. Towns in the Mojave Desert are few and far between; don't get stuck without gas and no place to get it.
- If your car becomes disabled, activate the hazard warning lights once safely out of the traffic lane. Do not abandon the car to go for help. Not only is it often a long walk to the nearest town or telephone, but high desert temperatures in the summer months bring a real threat of heat stroke—even a short walk could become dangerous.

**Note:** Desert driving often means that travelers must take "out of the ordinary" precautions in an emergency. For instance, pulling your car as far off the road as possible in an emergency is usually the most desirable action to take. Many areas of desert terrain do not offer a firm gravel surface off the asphalt shoulder, however, so be aware that driving onto a shoulder of soft sand may mean a tow truck will be required to get your car back onto the road.

When weather permits, motorists should follow normal emergency procedures: remain in your car, keep seat belt fastened and headrest properly positioned, keep doors locked and wait for assistance. In extreme desert heat these procedures will not be possible—even with the windows rolled down, the car will become unbearably hot. In such cases, seek out a shady area to wait for highway assistance, either in the shadow of the vehicle itself or in the shade of nearby vegetation. Do not leave pets or children in the car—they suffer the effects of the heat even more quickly than adults.

When faced with a disabled car, the best course of action the Auto Club can recommend is to wait for Highway Patrol assistance. Emergency call boxes are numerous along well-traveled highways, and cellular phones can be convenient tools for getting swift assistance. Highway Patrol officers also routinely make regular patrols of desert highways. Motorists should use extreme caution in accepting help from strangers.

effect on I-15, Los Angeles is only about a 5½-hour drive from Las Vegas; from San Diego it is about an hour farther. The San Francisco Bay Area is some 11 hours away by car, exclusive of stops. Although the 70 mph speed limit is in effect for almost all of the driving along I-15 in both California and Nevada, weather and road conditions often dictate a lower speed. For current highway conditions, call the Nevada Department of Transportation at (702) 486-3116 (recording). Drivers should also be alert to lower posted speed limits in populated areas.

**Laughlin** is approximately the same distance from Los Angeles as is Las Vegas. The routes from Los Angeles to both Las Vegas and Laughlin begin in a similar manner: I-10 east past Ontario, then north on I-15 to Barstow. At Barstow those bound for Las Vegas continue on I-15. For Laughlin, motorists take I-40 east across the Mojave Desert toward Needles. About 10 miles west of Needles motorists can take US 95 north 24 miles to SR 163 east 18 miles to Laughlin Civic Drive. Or about four miles west of Needles, there's an alternate route along Needles Highway (River Road) north to Laughlin. To get to the Arizona side of the river, SR 95 and Bullhead City, there's now a choice of three bridges (listed south to north): Needles, Veterans and Laughlin.

For **emergency road service**, AAA members may call **(800) AAA-HELP** in the USA and Canada; **(800) 955-4TDD** for the hearing impaired.

## Bus

Greyhound/Trailways offers service to Las Vegas from virtually any town in California and Nevada. Reservations are not accepted, and tickets can usually be purchased just prior to departure. In Las Vegas, Greyhound/Trailways uses the downtown bus terminal building at 200 South Main Street (at Carson Avenue); phone (800) 231-2222.

The routing for bus travelers to Laughlin-Bullhead City is through Needles, California, or Las Vegas, Nevada. From there both Greyhound/Trailways and K-T Services bus lines provide daily service to Laughlin; the trip takes about 2½ hours. Don Laughlin's Riverside Resort Hotel & Casino, South Tower, is the terminus in Laughlin for both bus lines. Both companies also serve Bullhead City, with pickups and drop-offs at the River Queen Motel, 125 Long Street. For more information, phone Greyhound/Trailways (702) 298-1934, (800) 231-2222; K-T Services (702) 644-2233.

## Train

Amtrak discontinued its *Desert Wind* train route in 1997, which provided service three times per week between Los Angeles and Las Vegas. However, Amtrak is considering plans to resume rail service between the two cities. Tentative plans call for a new train to begin operating in the fall of 1998. The Amtrak station in Las Vegas is located downtown, just behind Jackie Gaughan's Plaza Hotel at 1 North Main Street; phone (702) 386-6896. Total traveling time from Los Angeles to Las Vegas is seven hours. Pending the resumption of rail service, a Greyhound bus provides daily service between the Amtrak station in Las Vegas and Union Station in downtown Los Angeles. For fare and schedule information, call Amtrak at (800) 872-7245 (USA-RAIL). For reservations and help in arranging connecting trains or buses, contact any Travel Agency office of the Automobile Club of Southern California.

# Tourist Information Sources

*The chambers of commerce and visitor information bureaus listed below are resources for obtaining additional information about Las Vegas, Laughlin and surrounding areas. AAA/CSAA district offices provide travel services and publications, and highway information to Auto Club members.*

## Chambers of Commerce & Visitor Information Bureaus

**Boulder City Chamber of Commerce**
1305 Arizona St.
Boulder City, NV 89005
(702) 293-2034
Office hours: Mon.-Fri. 9 a.m.-5 p.m.

**Bullhead Area Chamber of Commerce**
1251 Hwy. 95
Bullhead City, AZ 86429
(520) 754-4121
Office hours: Mon.-Fri. 9 a.m.-5 p.m., Sat. 10 a.m.-2 p.m.

**Las Vegas Convention and Visitors Authority**
3150 Paradise Rd.
Las Vegas, NV 89109
(702) 892-7575, 892-0711
Office hours: Mon.-Fri. 8 a.m.-6 p.m., Sat.-Sun. 8 a.m.-5 p.m.

**Laughlin Visitors Bureau**
1555 S. Casino Dr.
Mailing address: P.O. Box 29849
Laughlin, NV 89029
(702) 298-3321
Office hours: Open daily 8 a.m.-5 p.m.

**Nevada Welcome Center**
100 Nevada Hwy.
Boulder City, NV 89005
Office hours: Open daily 8:30 a.m.-4:30 p.m.

## Auto Club District Offices

Automobile Club of Southern California district offices can help members in preparing a trip to anywhere in the world. For travel within the United States, Canada and Mexico, the Club can make reservations for lodging and transportation, and provide weather, routing and emergency road service information. The Auto Club's Travel Agency can make airline, train and package tour reservations for travel throughout the world.

Auto Club members can also take advantage of discounts on lodging, as indicated in the AAA *California/ Nevada TourBook,* available free to members. The Auto Club's *Member $aver* is published monthly and is a valuable source for seasonal discounts on events and points of interest.

The following AAA/California State Automobile Association district offices are located in the Las Vegas region.

**Henderson**
601 Whitney Ranch Dr., #A
Henderson, NV 89014
(702) 458-2323
Office hours: Mon.-Fri. 8:30 a.m.-5 p.m.

**Las Vegas**
3312 W. Charleston Blvd.
Las Vegas, NV 89102
(702) 870-9171
Office hours: Mon.-Fri. 8:30 a.m.-5 p.m.

# Lodging & Restaurants

*Despite the fact that **Las Vegas** has more than 100,000 rooms available, it is important to make reservations as far in advance as possible. "No vacancy" signs are constant reminders that the town operates at near capacity all year. During peak periods, a one-night reservation for Friday or Saturday night is difficult to obtain.*

*There are several things to be considered in addition to price when staying in Las Vegas. It is easier to obtain reservations to sellout celebrity shows when staying at the hotel where the performer is appearing. If convenient parking is important, a motel would probably be preferable to a hotel. Golf privileges, tennis and spa facilities may also be a consideration.*

***Laughlin** draws more than 50,000 visitors to its casinos on an average weekend, and holiday crowds can be even larger. While space is limited in Laughlin, additional lodging can also be found across the river in **Bullhead City, Arizona** (listings follow Nevada cities). Passenger ferries provide frequent service from parking lots on the Arizona side of the river to the various casinos on the Nevada side, and 24-hour shuttle bus service is available between the two cities.*

*Lodgings and restaurants are listed alphabetically by city and also include the communities of **Boulder City**, **Cottonwood Cove**, **Echo Bay-Lake Mead**, **Henderson** and **Primm**.*

*T*he lodging and restaurant properties listed in these pages have been inspected at least once in the past year by a trained representative of AAA. In surprise inspections, each property was found to meet AAA's extensive and detailed requirements for approval. These requirements are reflective of current industry standards and the expectations of the traveling public. Less than two-thirds of the lodging establishments open for business are listed in AAA publications.

Virtually all listings include AAA's "diamond" rating, reflecting the overall quality of the establishment. Many factors are considered in the process of determining the diamond rating. In lodging properties, the facility is first "classified" according to its physical design—is it a motel, a hotel, a resort, an apartment, etc. Since the various types of lodging establishments offer differing amenities and facilities, rating criteria are specific for each classification. For example, a motel, which typically offers a room with convenient

parking and little if any recreational or public facilities, is rated using criteria designed only for motel-type establishments—it is not compared to a hotel with its extensive public and meeting areas, or to a resort with its wide range of recreational facilities and programs. The diamonds do, however, represent standard levels of quality in all types of establishments.

There is no charge for a property to be listed in AAA publications. Many lodgings and restaurants, however, choose to advertise their AAA approval by displaying the ⊕ emblem on the premises and using it in their advertising. These properties are especially interested in serving AAA members.

Properties are listed alphabetically under the nearest town, with lodging facilities first and restaurants second. The location is given from the center of town or from the nearest major highway.

Nearly all lodging and restaurant facilities accept credit cards as forms of payment for services rendered. The following symbols are used to identify the specific cards accepted by each property.

| | |
|---|---|
| AE | American Express |
| CB | Carte Blanche |
| DI | Diners Club International |
| DS | Discover |
| JCB | Japanese credit card |
| MC | MasterCard |
| VI | VISA |

Some lodgings and restaurants listed in Auto Club publications have symbols indicating that they are accessible to individuals with disabilities. The criteria used in qualifying these listings are consistent with, but do not represent the full scope of, the Americans with Disabilities Act of 1990. AAA does not evaluate recreational facilities, banquet rooms or convention and meeting facilities for accessibility. Individuals with disabilities are urged to phone ahead to fully understand an establishment's facilities and accessibility.

In accommodations, a 🛇 indicates that at least one fully accessible guest room exists and that an individual with mobility impairments will be able to park and enter the building, register, and use at least one food and beverage outlet. For restaurants, the symbol indicates that parking, dining rooms and restrooms are accessible.

The 🖳 at the end of a lodging listing means that the following elements are provided: closed captioned decoders; text telephones; visual notification for fire alarms, incoming phone calls and door knocks; and phone amplification devices.

# Lodging

The following accommodations classifications appear in this book.

**Apartment**—Usually four or more stories with at least half the units equipped for housekeeping. Often in a vacation destination area. Units typically provide a full kitchen, living room and one or more bedrooms, but may be studio-type rooms with kitchen equipment in an alcove. May require a minimum stay and/or offer discounts for longer stays. This classification may also modify any of the other lodging types.

**Complex**—A combination of two or more kinds of lodgings.

**Condominium**—A destination property located in a resort area. Guest units consist of a bedroom, living room and kitchen. Kitchens are separate from bedrooms and are equipped with a stove, oven or microwave, refrigerator, cooking utensils and table settings for the maximum number of people occupying the unit. Linens and maid service are provided at least twice weekly. This classification may also modify any of the other lodging types.

**Hotel**—A multistory building usually including a coffee shop, dining room, lounge, room service, convenience shops, valet, laundry and full banquet/meeting facilities. Parking may be limited.

**Motel**—Usually one or two stories; food service, if any, consists of a limited facility or snack bar. Often has a pool or playground. Ample parking, usually adjacent to the guest room.

**Motor Inn**—Usually two or three stories, but may be a high-rise. Generally has recreation facilities, food service and ample parking. May have limited banquet/meeting facilities.

**Resort**—May be a destination in itself. Has a vacation atmosphere offering extensive recreational facilities for such specific interests as golf, tennis, fishing, etc. Rates may include meals under American or Modified American plans. This classification may also modify any of the other lodging types.

**Suite**—Units have one or more bedrooms and a living room, which may or may not be closed off from the bedrooms. This classification modifies other lodging types.

A property's **diamond rating** is not based on the room rate or any one specific aspect of its facilities or operations. Many factors are considered in calculating the rating, and certain minimum standards must be met in all inspection categories. If a property fails approval in just one category, it is not listed in Club publications. The inspection categories include housekeeping, maintenance, service, furnishings and decor. Guest comments received by AAA may also be reviewed in a property's approval/rating process.

These criteria apply to all properties listed in this publication:

- Clean and well-maintained facilities
- Hospitable staff
- Adequate parking
- A well-kept appearance
- Good quality bedding and comfortable beds with adequate illumination
- Good locks on all doors and windows
- Comfortable furnishings and decor
- Smoke detectors
- Adequate towels and supplies
- At least one comfortable easy chair with adequate illumination
- A desk or other writing surface with adequate illumination

Lodging ratings range from one to five diamonds and are defined below:

♦—Good but unpretentious. Establishments are functional. Clean and comfortable rooms must meet the basic needs of privacy and cleanliness.

♦♦—Shows noticeable enhancements in decor and/or quality of furnishings over those at the one-diamond level. May be recently constructed or an older property. Targets the needs of a budget-oriented traveler.

♦♦♦—Offers a degree of sophistication with additional amenities, services and facilities. There is a marked upgrade in services and comfort.

♦♦♦♦—Excellent properties displaying high levels of service and hospitality and offering a wide variety of amenities and upscale facilities, inside the room, on the grounds and in the common areas.

♦♦♦♦♦—Renowned for an exceptionally high degree of service, attractive and luxurious facilities and many extra amenities. Guest services are executed and presented in a flawless manner. Guests are pampered by a very professional, attentive staff. The property's facilities and operations set standards in hospitality and service.

**The diamond ratings shown in this publication are based on inspections done in 1996-97.**

Occasionally a property is listed without a rating, such as when an establishment was under construction or undergoing renovations at press time and a rating could not be determined.

**Room rates** shown in the listings are provided by each establishment's management for publication by the AAA. **All rates are subject to change.**

During special events or holiday periods, rates may exceed those published and special discounts or savings programs may not be honored. High-season rates are always shown; off-season rates are listed if they are substantially lower than the rest of the year. Rates are for typical rooms, not special units, and do not include taxes.

Many properties make special and discounted rates available exclusively to AAA members. Two publications list these rates: the AAA *TourBook*, which is published annually, and the Auto Club's *Member $aver,* a monthly newsletter featuring short-term rates and packages that offer a minimum of 20 percent off published rates for reservations made through the Auto Club. Both publications are available to AAA members at no charge through Auto Club offices.

Some properties offer discounts to senior citizens, or special rate periods such as weekly or monthly rentals. Inquiries as to the availability of any special discounts should be made at the time of registration. Typically, a property will allow a guest to take advantage of only one discount during his or her stay (i.e., a guest staying at a property offering both a AAA discount and a senior discount may choose only one of the two savings plans).

Each rate line gives the dates for which the rates are valid, the rates for one person (abbreviated 1P), two persons with one bed (2P/1B), two persons with two beds (2P/2B), and the rate for each extra person (XP) not included in the family rate. Figures following these abbreviations are the price(s) for the specified room and occupants. Most rates listed are European plan, which means that no meals are included in the

rate. Some lodgings' rates include breakfast [BP] or continental breakfast [CP]. A few properties offer an American Plan [AP], which includes three meals, or a Modified American Plan [MAP], which offers two meals, usually breakfast and dinner.

All baths have a combination tub and shower bath unless noted otherwise. Since nearly all establishments have air conditioning, telephones and color TV, only the absence of any of these items is noted in the listing. Movies are free unless indicated otherwise. Check-in time is shown only if it is after 3 p.m.; check-out time is shown only if it is before 10 a.m. Service charges are not shown unless they are $1 or more, or at least 5 percent of the room rate. If the pet acceptance policy varies within the establishment, no mention of pets is made; it is best to call ahead to verify specifics. By U.S. and Canada laws, pet restrictions do not apply to guide dogs. A heated pool is heated when it is reasonable to expect use of a pool. Outdoor pools may not be open in winter.

Reservations are always advisable in resort areas and may be the only way to assure obtaining the type of accommodations desired. Deposits are almost always required. Should plans change and reservations need to be canceled, be aware of the amount of notice required to receive a deposit refund.

Many properties welcome children in the same room with their parents at no additional charge; individual listings indicate if there is an age limit. There may be charges for additional equipment, such as roll-aways or cribs. Some properties offer a discount for guests ages 60 and over—be aware that the senior discount cannot usually be taken in conjunction with or in addition to other discounts. Many establishments have a minimum age requirement for renting rooms; in most cases the minimum age is 18, but at some properties the minimum age is 21.

Fire warning and protection equipment are indicated by the symbols Ⓓ (all guest rooms have smoke detectors) and Ⓢ (all guest rooms have sprinklers). Many properties have reserved rooms for nonsmokers; look for the ∅ symbol in the listing. If a smoke-free room is desired, be sure to indicate that request when making a reservation and upon registration.

## Restaurants

Restaurants listed in this publication have been found to be consistently good dining establishments. In metropolitan areas, where many restaurants are above average, some of those known for the superiority of their food, service and atmosphere are selected, as well as those offering a selection of quality food at moderate prices (including some cafeterias and family restaurants). In smaller communities, the restaurants considered to be the best in the area may be listed.

The type of cuisine featured at a dining establishment is used as a means of classification for restaurants. There are listings for Steakhouses and Continental cuisine as well as a range of ethnic foods, such as Chinese, Japanese, Italian and yes, American. Special menu types, such as early bird, a la carte, children's or Sunday brunch, are also listed. In many cases something is indicated about each restaurant's atmosphere and appropriate attire. The availability of alcoholic beverages is shown, as well as entertainment and dancing.

## ▼ Dining Out

Dining in **Las Vegas** is as varied as accommodations. Prices range from as little as $1 for breakfast to more than $50 for gourmet dinners. All of the large hotels have several places to eat, and many have themed dining rooms that feature regional or ethnic decor and food. Many coffee shops are open 24 hours a day. Buffets are available at almost every major hotel and offer diners a choice of three or four entrees, plus potatoes, vegetables, salads, desserts and a beverage for one price; buffet-style champagne brunches are offered at numerous hotels on weekends.

Similar to Las Vegas, all the large casino/hotels in **Laughlin** have several restaurants, some with themed dining rooms overlooking the river, that feature regional or ethnic food. Also, a number of restaurants and major fast-food franchise outlets can be found across the river in Bullhead City. Prices in Laughlin range from a low of about $2 for breakfast to a high of $30 for a gourmet dinner. Buffets are common and range in price from $5 to $7; buffet breakfasts are priced from $2 to $3.50; and lunches are priced similarly.

Price ranges are for an average, complete meal without alcoholic beverage. Taxes and tips are not included.

Restaurant ratings are applied to two categories of operational style—full-service eating establishments and self-service, family dining operations such as cafeterias or buffets.

♦—Good but unpretentious dishes. Table settings are usually simple and may include paper place mats and napkins. Alcoholic beverage service, if any, may be limited to beer and wine. Usually informal with an atmosphere conducive to family dining.

♦♦—More extensive menus representing more complex food preparation and, usually, a wider variety of alcoholic beverages. The atmosphere is appealing and suitable for either family or adult dining. Service may be casual, but host or hostess seating can be expected. Table settings may include tablecloths and cloth napkins.

♦♦♦—Extensive or specialized menus and more complex cuisine preparation requiring that a professional chef contribute to either a formal dining experience or a special family meal. Cloth table linens, above-average quality table settings, a skilled service staff and an inviting decor should all be provided. Generally, the wine list includes representatives of the best domestic and foreign wine-producing regions.

♦♦♦♦—An appealing ambiance is often enhanced by fresh flowers and fine furnishings. The overall sophistication and formal atmosphere visually create a dining experience more for adults than for families. A wine steward presents an extensive list of the best wines. A smartly attired, highly skilled staff is capable of describing how any dish is prepared. Elegant silverware, china and correct glassware are typical. The menu includes creative dishes prepared from fresh ingredients by a chef who frequently has international training. Eye-appealing desserts are offered at tableside.

♦♦♦♦♦—A world-class operation with even more luxury and sophistication than four-diamond restaurants. A proportionally large staff, expert in preparing tableside delicacies, provides flawless service. Tables are set with impeccable linens, silver and crystal glassware.

# Boulder City

## Lodging

**BEST WESTERN LIGHTHOUSE INN** 🆎      ♦♦ Motel
*1 mi E via SR 93; 110 Ville Dr, 89005.*
*(702) 293-6444; FAX (702) 293-6547.*

| | | | |
|---|---|---|---|
| Fri-Sat [CP] | 1P $68-85 | 2P/1B $68-85 | 2P/2B $68-85 |
| Sun-Thu [CP] | 1P $58-75 | 2P/1B $58-75 | 2P/2B $58-75 |

XP $10. Reservation deposit required. Some rooms with view of Lake Mead. 3 stories; exterior corridors. No elevator. 70 rooms. Cable TV, coffeemakers, movies; fee for refrigerators. Pool, whirlpool. Coin laundry. No pets. AE, CB, DI, DS, MC, VI. 🄳 🅂 ⊘

**EL RANCHO BOULDER MOTEL** 🆎      ♦♦ Motel
*On US 93 at 725 Nevada Hwy, 89005.*
*(702) 293-1085; FAX (702) 293-3021.*

| | | | |
|---|---|---|---|
| All year | 1P $55-70 | 2P/1B $60-70 | 2P/2B $60-100 |

XP $10. Reservation deposit required; 7-day refund notice. Spanish-style decor. Attractive landscaped grounds. 2 stories; exterior corridors. 39 rooms; 7 2-bedroom units. Cable TV, movies, refrigerators. Pool. No pets. AE, DI, DS, MC, VI. Coffee shop nearby. 🄳 ⊘

**SANDS MOTEL** 🆎      ♦ Motel
*On US 93 at 809 Nevada Hwy, 89005.*
*(702) 293-2589.*

All year          1P $32-38          2P/1B $38-44          2P/2B $44-52
XP $6; ages 12 and under stay free. Credit card guarantee; 3-day refund notice. Some small units. 1 story; exterior corridors. 25 rooms; 2 2-bedroom units. Cable TV, movies, refrigerators; some shower baths. No pets. AE, CB, DI, DS, MC, VI. Ⓓ Ⓧ

# Cottonwood Cove

## Lodging

**COTTONWOOD COVE MOTEL** ⏹            ♦♦ Motel
*Between Las Vegas and Needles; 14 mi E of Searchlight off US 95; Box 1000, 89046.*
*(702) 297-1464; FAX (702) 297-1464.*
3/15-10/31          1P $95          2P/1B $95          2P/2B $90
11/1-3/14           1P $60          2P/1B $60          2P/2B $55
XP $8. Reservation deposit reqired; 5-day refund notice. Overlooking Lake Mohave. 1 story; exterior corridors. 24 rooms. Cable TV, movies, rental VCPs; some shower baths. Swimming, fishing, water-skiing. Beach, boat ramp, marina; fee for houseboats, power boats and equipment. Coin laundry. No pets. AE, DS, MC, VI. Coffee shop, 7 am-8 pm; 9/6-5/27 8 am-6 pm; $5-14. Ⓓ Ⓧ

# Echo Bay-Lake Mead

## Lodging

**ECHO BAY RESORT** ⏹            ♦♦ Motor Inn
*On Lake Mead, 4 mi E of SR 167; Overton, 89040.*
*(702) 394-4000; FAX (702) 394-4180.*
All year          1P $69          2P/1B $74          2P/2B $69-84
XP $6. Reservation deposit required; 3-day refund notice. Some rooms with lake view; many with balcony or patio. 2 stories; interior corridors. 52 rooms; 4 family rooms, $84 for up to 4 persons. Pay movies. Fishing, swimming, water-skiing. Marina, houseboats, rental boats. Coin laundry. Pets, $5; $25 deposit. Meeting rooms. MC, VI. Restaurant, 7 am-8:30 pm; 5/1-9/30, 6 am-9:30 pm; $8-17; cocktails and lounge. Ⓓ Ⓧ

# Henderson

## Lodging

**BEST WESTERN LAKE MEAD MOTEL** ⏹        ♦♦ Motel
*Exit US 93/95 at Lake Mead Dr, ½ mi E on SR 146; 85 W Lake Mead Dr, 89015.*
*(702) 564-1712; FAX (702) 564-7642.*
Fri-Sat          1P $75-99          2P/1B $75-99          2P/2B $75-99
Sun-Thu          1P $43-51          2P/1B $48-56          2P/2B $48-56
XP $5; ages 12 and under stay free. 2 stories; exterior corridors. 59 rooms. Cable TV, movies; some refrigerators. Small pool. Coin laundry. No pets. AE, CB, DI, DS, MC, VI. Ⓓ Ⓢ Ⓧ

**THE RESERVE HOTEL CASINO** ⏹        Under construction-Hotel
*Exit US 93/95 at Lake Mead Dr, 777 Lake Mead Dr, 89015.*
*(702) 558-7000; FAX (702) 558-7008.*
Fri-Sat          1P $75-99          2P/1B $75-99          2P/2B $75-99
Sun-Thu          1P $43-51          2P/1B $48-56          2P/2B $48-56
Reservation deposit required. Senior discount. 8 stories; interior corridors. 224 rooms. Cable TV. Pool. No pets. AE, CB, DI, DS, JCB, MC. Dining room; restaurant; $7-20. Ⓓ Ⓢ Ⓧ

# Las Vegas

## Lodging

### ALEXIS PARK RESORT HOTEL    ♦♦♦ Resort Hotel
*I-15 exit E Tropicana Av, 2 blocks W of UNLV, 2 mi S of Convention Center; 375 E Harmon Av, 89109.*
*(702) 796-3300; FAX (702) 796-4334.*

| | | | |
|---|---|---|---|
| All year | 1P $99-585 | 2P/1B $99-585 | 2P/2B $99-585 |

XP $15. Check in 4 pm. Spacious landscaped grounds. 2 stories; exterior corridors. 980 rooms; 484 2-bedroom units; 12 2-bedroom, 2-story suites, $350-1150 for up to 4 persons. Cable TV, pay movies, honor bars, refrigerators; some air conditioning, radios, phones, data ports, whirlpools, gas fireplaces. 3 pools; saunas, whirlpools, 2 lighted tennis courts, putting green; fee for health club and massage. Valet parking. No pets. PC; secretarial services. Business center; meeting rooms. AE, CB, DI, DS, JCB, MC, VI. Restaurant; coffee shop; 6 am-midnight, $12-80; cocktails and lounge; 24-hr room service; entertainment.  Ⓓ Ⓢ ∅ 🖾

### ARIZONA CHARLIE'S HOTEL    ⏣   ♦♦ Motor Inn
*1 mi NW of I-15; Charleston Bl exit; 740 S Decatur Bl at Evergreen Av, 89107.*
*(702) 258-5111; FAX (702) 258-5192.*

| | | | |
|---|---|---|---|
| Fri-Sat | 1P $69 | 2P/1B $69 | 2P/2B $69 |
| Sun-Thu | 1P $48 | 2P/1B $48 | 2P/2B $48 |

XP $4; ages 12 and under stay free. No Sat arrivals. 2-night minimum stay weekends. Old West atmosphere. 7 stories; interior corridors. 257 rooms; luxury-level rooms. Some shower baths, roll-in showers, refrigerators, radios. Small pool, whirlpool. Airport transportation. Valet laundry. No pets. Meeting rooms. AE, CB, DI, DS, MC, VI. 2 restaurants; coffee shop; $30-45; buffet, $5; casino, 24 hrs; cocktail lounge. Ⓓ Ⓢ ∅ 🖾 🖾

### BALLY'S LAS VEGAS    ⏣   ♦♦♦ Hotel
*4½ mi S on the Strip at 3645 Las Vegas Bl S; Box 96505, 89109.*
*(702) 739-4111; FAX (702) 739-4405.*

| | | | |
|---|---|---|---|
| All year | 1P $99-220 | 2P/1B $99-220 | 2P/2B $99-220 |

XP $15; ages 18 and under stay free. Reservation deposit required. Package plans. Rooms in 2 towers connected by casino and public areas. 26 stories; interior corridors. 2814 rooms; 1- and 2-bedroom suites, $450; luxury-level rooms. Cable TV, pay movies, data ports; some refrigerators, whirlpools, roll-in showers. Pool, sauna, steam room, whirlpool, 8 lighted tennis courts; fee for health club and massage. Valet parking. Valet laundry. No pets. Conference facilities, convention-oriented. AE, DI, DS, JCB, MC, VI. 4 restaurants; 2 24-hr coffee shops; $8-34; buffet, $15, 4:30-10 pm; casino; cocktails and lounge; name entertainment. Ⓓ Ⓢ ∅

### BARBARY COAST HOTEL    ♦♦♦ Hotel
*1⅛ mi S on the Strip; 3595 Las Vegas Bl S; Box 19030, 89132.*
*(702) 737-7111; FAX (702) 737-6304.*

| | | | |
|---|---|---|---|
| Fri-Sat | 1P $100 | 2P/1B $100 | 2P/2B $100 |
| Sun-Thu | 1P $ 75 | 2P/1B $ 75 | 2P/2B $ 75 |

XP $5; ages 18 and under stay free. Reservation deposit required. Gay '90s decor, including large Tiffany-style stained glass mural. 4 stories; interior corridors. 200 rooms; 12 suites, $200-350 for up to 2 persons. Cable TV, free and pay movies, data ports; some refrigerators, roll-in showers; fee for whirlpools. Valet laundry. No pets. AE, CB, DI, DS, JCB, MC, VI. Restaurant; 24-hr coffee shop; $7-20; casino; cocktails. Ⓓ Ⓢ ∅

### BARCELONA MOTEL    ⏣   ♦♦ Motor Inn
*7 mi NE; ½ mi from Nellis AFB, I-15 exit 48E; 5011 E Craig Rd, 89115.*
*(702) 644-6300; FAX (702) 644-6510.*

| | | | |
|---|---|---|---|
| Fri-Sat | 1P $50 | 2P/1B $55 | 2P/2B $65 |
| Sun-Thu | 1P $40 | 2P/1B $45 | 2P/2B $45 |

XP $5; ages 12 and under stay free. Early check-in and late check-out. 2 stories; exterior corridors. 177 rooms. Pay movies; fee for safes, microwaves; some kitchens (no utensils), refrigerators, shower baths, roll-in showers. Small pool, whirlpool. Coin laundry. No pets. AE, DI, DS, MC, VI. 24-hr coffee shop; $6-10; small casino; cocktails; entertainment. [D] ⊘

### BEST WESTERN HERITAGE INN ⬤ ♦♦♦ Motel
*3 blocks W of jct I-15 and Tropicana Av at 4975 S Valley View, 89103.*
*(702) 798-7736; (702) 798-5951.*

| | | | |
|---|---|---|---|
| All year [CP] | 1P $59-110 | 2P/1B $59-110 | 2P/2B $69-140 |

Reservation deposit required. 3 stories; interior corridors. No elevators. 59 rooms; 6 efficiencies, 3 kitchens. Cable TV, pay movies; some shower baths, refrigerators; fee for whirlpools. Heated indoor pool. Coin laundry. Pets. AE, CB, DI, DS, JCB, MC. Restaurants nearby. [D] [S] ⊘

### BEST WESTERN MAIN STREET INN ⬤ ♦♦ Motor Inn
*I-15 northbound, exit 43E; I-15 southbound, exit 44E; 1000 N Main St, 89101.*
*(702) 382-3455; FAX (702) 382-1428.*

| | | | |
|---|---|---|---|
| Fri-Sat | 1P $61-110 | 2P/1B $66-110 | 2P/2B $61-110 |
| Sun-Thu 5/26-9/1 | 1P $51-110 | 2P/1B $56-110 | 2P/2B $51-110 |
| Sun-Thu 9/2-5/25 | 1P $50-100 | 2P/1B $52-100 | 2P/2B $50-100 |

XP $8; ages 12 and under stay free. Reservation deposit required. Near downtown convention center. 2-3 stories; exterior corridors. 91 rooms. Fee for refrigerators. Small pool. Coin laundry. Small pets only, $8. Meeting rooms. AE, CB, DI, DS, MC, VI. 24-hr restaurant; $8-12; cocktail lounge. [D] ⊘

### BEST WESTERN MARDI GRAS INN ⬤ ♦♦ Motor Inn
*½ mi S of convention center; 3500 Paradise Rd, 89109.*
*(702) 731-2020; FAX (702) 733-6994.*

| | | | |
|---|---|---|---|
| 1/3-5/31 & 9/1-11/30 | 1P $35- 99 | 2P/1B $35- 99 | 2P/2B $35- 99 |
| 6/1-8/31 | 1P $30- 99 | 2P/1B $30- 99 | 2P/2B $30- 99 |
| 12/1-12/28 | 1P $25- 59 | 2P/1B $25- 59 | 2P/2B $25- 59 |
| 12/29-1/2 | 1P $50-120 | 2P/1B $50-120 | 2P/2B $50-120 |

XP $6 12/29-11/30; ages 18 and under stay free. Reservation deposit required. Phone charge $1.50/day. 3 stories; exterior corridors. 314 rooms. Cable TV, free and pay movies, refrigerators, coffeemakers, data ports; phone charge $1.50 per day. Pool, whirlpool; sun deck. Airport transportation. Coin laundry. No pets. Conference facilities. AE, CB, DI, DS, JCB, MC, VI. 24-hr restaurant; $9-14; slot casino; cocktails. [D] ⊘

### BEST WESTERN McCARRAN INN ⬤ ♦♦ Motel
*I-15 exit Tropicana E toward McCarran International Airport; 4970 Paradise Rd, 89119.*
*(702) 798-5530; FAX (702) 798-7627.*

| | | | |
|---|---|---|---|
| Fri-Sat [CP] | 1P $69-139 | 2P/1B $69-139 | 2P/2B $69-139 |
| Sun-Thu [CP] | 1P $49-129 | 2P/1B $49-129 | 2P/2B $49-129 |

XP $7; ages 17 and under stay free. Early check-in and late check-out. Senior discount. Located directly across from airport. 3 stories; interior corridors. 99 rooms. Cable TV, pay movies; some coffeemakers. Pool. Airport and area transportation within 2 mi. Coin laundry. No pets. AE, CB, DI, DS, JCB, MC, VI. [D] ⊘

### BEST WESTERN NELLIS MOTOR INN ⬤ ♦♦ Motel
*7 mi NE, ³/₁₀ mi from Nellis AFB; from I-15, exit 48E; 5330 E Craig Rd, 89115.*
*(702) 643-6111; FAX (702) 643-8553.*

| | | | |
|---|---|---|---|
| Fri-Sat 5/25-9/3 | 1P $53 | 2P/1B $59 | 2P/2B $59 |
| Sun-Thu 5/25-9/3 | 1P $43 | 2P/1B $49 | 2P/2B $49 |
| Fri-Sat 9/4-5/24 | 1P $49 | 2P/1B $47 | 2P/2B $47 |
| Sun-Thu 9/4-5/24 | 1P $41 | 2P/1B $47 | 2P/2B $47 |

XP $6; ages 12 and under stay free. Reservation deposit required. Senior discount. 2 stories; exterior corridors. 52 rooms. Cable TV, coffeemakers; some refrigerators. Pool, playground. Coin laundry. Pets, $5; $50 deposit. AE, DI, DS, JCB, MC, VI. Coffee shop nearby. Ⓓ ⊘

### BEST WESTERN PARKVIEW INN  ⬥⬥  ♦♦ Motel
*8 blocks N on US 91 and 93; 905 Las Vegas Bl N, 89101.*
*(702) 385-1213; FAX (702) 382-1428.*

| | | | |
|---|---|---|---|
| Fri-Sat | 1P $54-100 | 2P/1B $58-100 | 2P/2B $64-100 |
| Sun-Thu 5/26-9/6 | 1P $46- 86 | 2P/1B $50- 86 | 2P/2B $56- 86 |
| Sun-Thu 9/7-5/25 | 1P $44- 68 | 2P/1B $48- 68 | 2P/2B $52- 68 |

XP $8; ages 12 and under stay free. Reservation deposit required. Senior discount. 2 stories; exterior corridors. 56 rooms. Small pool. Coin laundry. Small pets only, $8. AE, CB, DI, DS, MC, VI. Ⓓ ⊘

### BLAIR HOUSE SUITES  ⬥⬥  ♦♦ Apartment Motel
*Exit I-15 at Sahara E, ½ mi to Paradise Rd, S to Desert Inn Rd, W ¼ mi; 344 E Desert Inn Rd, 89109.*
*(702) 792-2222; FAX (702) 792-9042.*

| | | | |
|---|---|---|---|
| Fri-Sat | 1P $125 | 2P/1B $125 | 2P/2B $125 |
| Sun-Thu | 1P $ 65 | 2P/1B $ 65 | 2P/2B $ 65 |

XP $10; ages 17 and under stay free. Early check-in and late check-out. 3 stories; exterior corridors. 224 rooms. Cable TV, VCPs, pay movies, kitchens, data ports. Pool, whirlpool. Area and airport transportation. Coin laundry. No pets. Conference facilities. AE, CB, DI, DS, MC, VI. Ⓓ Ⓢ ⊘

### CALIFORNIA HOTEL  ♦♦ Hotel
*In downtown casino center area at 1st and Ogden; Box 630, 89125.*
*(702) 385-1222; FAX (702) 388-2660.*

| | | | |
|---|---|---|---|
| Fri-Sat | 1P $50-80 | 2P/1B $50-80 | 2P/2B $50-80 |
| Sun-Thu | 1P $40-65 | 2P/1B $40-65 | 2P/2B $40-65 |

XP $5. Reservation deposit required. "Aloha"-style decor. 11-13 stories; interior corridors. 781 rooms. Cable TV, pay movies, safes; some refrigerators, shower baths, roll-in showers. Pool, whirlpool open 4/1-10/31; recreation program. Valet parking. No pets. Meeting rooms. AE, CB, DI, DS, MC, VI. 2 restaurants; 24-hr coffee shop; $8-25; casino; cocktails and lounge. Ⓓ Ⓢ ⊘ ▨

### CARRIAGE HOUSE  ⬥⬥  ♦♦♦ Condo Hotel
*1 block E off the Strip; 105 E Harmon Av, 89109.*
*(702) 798-1020; FAX (702) 798-1020.*

| | | | |
|---|---|---|---|
| All year | 1P $125-345 | 2P/1B $125-345 | 2P/2B ... |

Reservation deposit required. 9 stories; interior corridors. 154 rooms; 15 2-bedroom units, $275-525 for 2-8 persons; 41 efficiencies, 113 kitchens. Cable TV, movies, microwaves; some VCPs; shower baths; fee for safes. Pool, whirlpool, 1 lighted tennis court. Area transportation to Strip, convention center and airport. Coin laundry. No pets. AE, DI, DS, MC, VI. Restaurant, 7-10 am and 5-10 pm; Sat-Sun to midnight; $15-30; cocktail lounge. Ⓓ Ⓢ ⊘ **(See ad next page.)**

**CENTER STRIP INN** (AAA)      ♦ Motel

*I-15 exit Flamingo Rd E, S on the Strip; 3688 Las Vegas Bl S, 89109.*
*(702) 739-6066; FAX (702) 736-2521.*

| | | | |
|---|---|---|---|
| Fri-Sat | 1P $50-151 | 2P/1B $60-250 | 2P/2B $60-250 |
| Sun-Thu | 1P $30- 70 | 2P/1B $40- 99 | 2P/2B $40- 99 |

XP $10. Reservation deposit required. 2-5 stories; exterior corridors. 152 rooms; 4 2-bedroom units; spa/steam rooms, Sun-Thu $69-99, Fri and Sat $89-149. Cable TV, movies, refrigerators, safes, VCPs; some microwaves, whirlpools. Coin laundry. Pool. Small pets only, $10 deposit. AE, DI, DS, MC, VI. Coffee shop nearby. Ⓓ ∅

**CIRCUS CIRCUS HOTEL**      ♦♦ Hotel

*2½ mi S on the Strip at 2880 Las Vegas Bl S; Box 14967, 89114.*
*(702) 734-0410; FAX (702) 734-5897.*

| | | | |
|---|---|---|---|
| All year | 1P $39-89 | 2P/1B $39-89 | 2P/2B $39-89 |

XP $10. Reservation deposit required. Circus entertainment 11 am-midnight; Grand Slam Canyon. Hotel towers; motel rooms in 3-story building. 2-29 stories; interior corridors. 3744 rooms. Safes, cable TV, pay movies, rental VCPs, data ports; some radios, refrigerators, shower baths, roll-in showers. 3 pools, whirlpool. Valet parking. Valet laundry. No pets. AE, CB, DI, DS, MC, VI. 3 restaurants; 2 24-hr coffee shops; $7-25; buffet, $5; casino; cocktails. Ⓓ Ⓢ ∅ ⓖ ⓩ

**COMFORT INN** (AAA)      ♦♦♦ Motel

*I-15 exit Cheyenne West; 910 E Cheyenne Av, 89030.*
*(702) 399-1500.*

| | | | |
|---|---|---|---|
| Fri-Sat [CP] | 1P $69-79 | 2P/1B $69-79 | 2P/2B $69-79 |
| Sun-Thu [CP] | 1P $59-69 | 2P/1B $59-69 | 2P/2B $59-69 |

XP $10; ages 18 and under stay free. 2 stories; interior corridors. 59 rooms; 3 kitchens. Cable TV, movies; some shower baths, microwaves, refrigerators; fee for whirlpools. Pool, whirlpool, sauna. Coin laundry. Pets at manager's discretion. AE, CB, DI, DS, MC, VI. Coffee shop nearby. Ⓓ ∅

**COMFORT INN CENTRAL** (AAA)      ♦♦ Motel

*From I-15 exit Flamingo Rd E at Koval Rd; 211 E Flamingo Rd, 89109.*
*(702) 733-7800; FAX (702) 733-7353.*

| | | | |
|---|---|---|---|
| Fri-Sat [CP] | 1P $65 | 2P/1B $75 | 2P/2B $85 |
| Sun-Thu [CP] | 1P $55 | 2P/1B $65 | 2P/2B $75 |

XP $10; ages 16 and under stay free. Reservation deposit required. 2 stories; exterior corridors. 121 rooms; 4 2-bedroom units. Cable TV, free and pay movies. Pool. No pets. AE, CB, DI, DS, JCB, MC, VI. Restaurant nearby. Ⓓ ∅

## COMFORT INN SOUTH   (AAA)       ♦♦ Motel
*½ mi E of I-15, Tropicana Av exit; 5075 S Koval Ln, 89109.*
*(702) 736-3600; FAX (702) 736-0726.*

| | | | |
|---|---|---|---|
| Fri-Sat [CP] | 1P $80 | 2P/1B $80 | 2P/2B $80 |
| Sun-Thu [CP] | 1P $48 | 2P/1B $57 | 2P/2B $57 |

XP $5; ages 18 and under stay free. Reservation deposit required. 2 stories; exterior corridors. 106 rooms; comfortable rooms. Cable TV, free and pay movies. Small pool. Valet laundry. No pets. AE, CB, DI, DS, JCB, MC, VI. (D) ⊘

## COURTYARD BY MARRIOTT       ♦♦♦ Motor Inn
*3 blocks E of the Strip, 1 block to convention center; 3275 Paradise Rd, 89109.*
*(702) 791-3600; FAX (702) 796-7981.*

| | | | |
|---|---|---|---|
| All year | 1P $80-135 | 2P/1B $80-135 | 2P/2B $80-135 |

Rates for up to 5 persons. 3 stories; interior corridors. 149 rooms. Free and pay movies, refrigerators. Pool, whirlpool, exercise room. Airport transportation. Coin laundry. No pets. Meeting rooms. AE, CB, DI, DS, JCB, MC, VI. Dining room, 6:30 am-10 pm; $8-16; cocktails. (D) (S) ⊘

## CROWNE PLAZA   (AAA)       ♦♦♦ Motor Inn
*Exit I-15 Flamingo, ½ mi E to Paradise, S to 4255 S Paradise Rd, 89109.*
*(702) 369-4400; FAX (702) 369-3770.*

| | | | |
|---|---|---|---|
| All year | 1P $125-185 | 2P/1B $125-185 | 2P/2B $125-185 |

XP $15; ages 18 and under stay free. Atrium lobby, vibrant colors, cascading fountains. 6 stories; interior corridors. 201 rooms; luxury-level rooms. Cable TV, free and pay movies, refrigerators, coffeemakers; fee for microwaves. Pool, whirlpool, sauna, exercise room. Area, Strip, convention center and airport transportation. Valet laundry. Pets, $200 deposit; on first floor only. Secretarial services, conference facilities. AE, CB, DI, DS, JCB, MC, VI. Restaurant, 6 am-10 pm; $8-16; cocktails and lounge. (D) (S) ⊘ (占) (⇗)

## DAYS INN-AIRPORT       ♦♦ Motel
*Exit I-15 at E Tropicana Av, 1⅛ mi E to Paradise Rd, ½ mi S to 5125 Swenson St, 89119.*
*(702) 740-4040; FAX (702) 736-8295.*

| | | | |
|---|---|---|---|
| Fri-Sat | 1P $65-145 | 2P/1B $65-145 | 2P/2B $65-145 |
| Sun-Thu | 1P $45-125 | 2P/1B $45-125 | 2P/2B $45-125 |

Senior discount. 2 stories; exterior corridors, 183 rooms. Cable TV. Pool. No pets. Area, Strip and airport transportation. AE, CB, DI, DS, MC, VI. (D) ⊘

## DAYS INN DOWNTOWN   (AAA)       ♦♦ Motel
*On US 93 and 95 business rte; 707 E Fremont St, 89101.*
*(702) 388-1400; FAX (702) 388-9622.*

| | | | |
|---|---|---|---|
| Fri-Sat 1/2-11/14 & | | | |
| Fri-Sat 11/22-12/26 | 1P $ 50-120 | 2P/1B $ 60-120 | 2P/2B $ 60-120 |
| Sun-Thu 1/2-11/14 & | | | |
| Sun-Thu 11/22-12/26 | 1P $ 36-100 | 2P/1B $ 46-100 | 2P/2B $ 46-100 |
| 11/15-11/21 & | | | |
| 12/27-1/1 | 1P $110-150 | 2P/1B $110-150 | 2P/2B $120-175 |

XP $10; ages 16 and under stay free. Early check-in and late check-out. Senior discount. 3 stories; exterior corridors. 147 rooms; few small rooms, some large; 7 1-bedroom suites, $60-120. Cable TV, rental VCPs, pay movies. Pool. No pets. AE, CB, DI, DS, JCB, MC, VI. Restaurant, 7 am-9 pm, Sat and Sun to noon; culinary training facility, motel guests only. (D) ⊘

## THE DESERT INN       ♦♦♦♦ Resort Complex
*On the Strip; I-15 NB exit E Flamingo Av, SB exit E Sahara Av; 3145 Las Vegas Bl S, 89109.*
*(702) 733-4444; FAX (702) 733-4774.*

| | | | |
|---|---|---|---|
| All year [CP] | 1P $195-275 | 2P/1B $195-275 | 2P/2B $195-275 |

XP $35; ages 17 and under stay free. Reservation deposit required; 3-day refund notice.

Attractive landscaped grounds. 14 stories; interior corridors. 715 rooms; 40 whirlpool suites, $1500-5000 for up to 2 persons. Cable TV, pay movies; some refrigerators, whirlpools. Heated pool, whirlpools, sauna, jogging, 10 lighted tennis courts; fee for 18 holes golf, health club, spa. Valet parking. Valet laundry. No pets. Conference facilities. AE, DI, DS, JCB, MC, VI. 3 dining rooms, coffee shop; 24 hrs; $12-65; 24-hr room service; cocktails and lounge; name entertainment; also Monte Carlo Restaurant, see separate listing. Sheraton Hotels & Motor Inns. D S ⊘

### ECONO LODGE-DOWNTOWN ⓐⓐⓐ ♦ Motel
*Exit I-15 downtown casino center; 520 S Casino Center Bl, 89101.*
*(702) 384-8211; FAX (702) 384-8580.*

| | | | |
|---|---|---|---|
| Fri-Sat | 1P $45 | 2P/1B $45 | 2P/2B $55 |
| Sun-Thu | 1P $35 | 2P/1B $35 | 2P/2B $45 |

XP $8. Reservation deposit required. 3 stories; interior corridors. 48 rooms; 4 1-bedroom apartments, $69-95 for up to 4 persons; 4 kitchens, no utensils. Refrigerators, coffeemakers, movies. Coin laundry. No pets. AE, CB, DI, DS, JCB, MC, VI. D ⊘

### EMERALD SPRINGS-HOLIDAY INN ⓐⓐⓐ ♦♦♦ Motor Inn
*I-15 exit E Flamingo Rd; 325 E Flamingo Rd, 89109.*
*(702) 732-9100; FAX (702) 731-9784.*

| | | | |
|---|---|---|---|
| All year | 1P $72-175 | 2P/1B $72-175 | 2P/2B $72-175 |

XP $15; ages 18 and under stay free. Reservation deposit required. 3-day refund notice. Senior discount. 3 stories; interior corridors. 150 rooms; suites, $99-250 for up to 2 persons; 16 suites with wet bar and whirlpool tub. Cable TV, coffeemakers, free and pay movies, refrigerators, rental VCPs, data ports; some microwaves. Pool, whirlpool, exercise room. Area, Strip (7 am-11 pm) and airport transportation. Valet laundry. No pets. Secretarial services. Conference facilities. AE, CB, DI, DS, JCB, MC, VI. Restaurant, 6:30 am-10 pm; Fri and Sat to 11 pm; $10-20; cocktails and lounge. D S ⊘

### EXCALIBUR HOTEL & CASINO ♦♦♦ Hotel
*I-15 exit E Tropicana Ave; 3850 Las Vegas Bl S; Box 96778, 89193.*
*(702) 597-7777; FAX (702) 597-7009.*

| | | | |
|---|---|---|---|
| All year | 1P $55-220 | 2P/1B $55-220 | 2P/2B $55-220 |

XP $10; ages 17 and under stay free. Medieval castle theme. 28 stories; interior corridors. 4017 rooms. Shower baths, pay movies; some roll-in showers; fee for refrigerators, whirlpools. Pool, whirlpool, arcade. Valet parking. Valet laundry. No pets. AE, CB, DI, DS, MC, VI. Dining room; 5 restaurants; 24-hr coffee shop; $5-30; buffet, $6; casino; cocktails and lounge; 24-hr room service; entertainment. D S ⊘ ♿ 🖭

### FAIRFIELD INN BY MARRIOTT ♦♦ Motel
*I-15 exit E Flamingo Rd; 3 blocks N of convention center; 3850 Paradise Rd, 89109.*
*(702) 791-0899; FAX (702) 791-0899.*

| | | | |
|---|---|---|---|
| 2/1-6/1 [CP] | 1P $48 | 2P/1B $54 | 2P/2B $54 |
| 6/2-8/31 [CP] | 1P $44 | 2P/1B $50 | 2P/2B $20 |
| 9/1-1/31 [CP] | 1P $56-79 | 2P/1B $56-79 | 2P/2B $56-79 |

XP $3; ages 18 and under stay free. Rates for up to 4 persons. Senior discount. Large lobby with many tables and chairs; comfortable rooms. 4 stories; interior corridors. 129 rooms. Cable TV, free and pay movies. Pool, whirlpool. Airport transportation. No pets. Meeting rooms. AE, DI, DS, MC, VI. Restaurant nearby. D S ⊘ 🖭

### FIESTA CASINO HOTEL ♦♦ Motor Inn
*3 mi N of downtown at 2400 N Rancho Dr, 89130.*
*(702) 631-7000; FAX (702) 631-7070.*

| | | | |
|---|---|---|---|
| All year | 1P $39 | 2P/1B $42 | 2P/2B $45 |

XP $5. 4 stories; interior corridors. 100 rooms. Cable TV. No pets. AE, DI, DS, MC, VI. Restaurant & coffee shop, 24 hrs; $9-18; cocktails and lounge. D S ⊘

**FLAMINGO HILTON-LAS VEGAS** 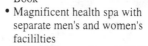 ♦♦♦ Hotel

*From I-15, exit Flamingo Rd E, then N on the Strip; 3555 Las Vegas Bl S, 89109.*
*(702) 733-3111; FAX (702) 733-3528.*

| | | | |
|---|---|---|---|
| All year | 1P $69-279 | 2P/1B $69-279 | 2P/2B $69-279 |

XP $20; ages 18 and under stay free. 2-28 stories; interior corridors. 3642 rooms; suites, $250-5800 for up to 2 persons. Cable TV, pay movies; some safes, roll-in showers; rental refrigerators. 2 pools, water slide, whirlpools; fee for 4 lighted tennis courts, health club, massage. Valet parking. Valet laundry. No pets. Conference facilities. AE, DI, DS, MC, VI. 5 restaurants; cafeteria; 24-hr coffee shop; $7-20; buffet, $5-8; casino; cocktails and lounge; 24-hr room service; entertainment. Ⓓ Ⓢ ⊘ **(See ad below.)**

**FOUR QUEENS HOTEL** 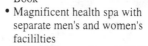 ♦♦ Hotel

*In the downtown casino center area; 202 Fremont St, 89101.*
*(702) 385-4011; FAX (702) 387-5123.*

| | | | |
|---|---|---|---|
| Fri-Sat | 1P $75 | 2P/1B $75 | 2P/2B $75 |
| Sun-Thu 5/26-8/28 & Sun-Thu 11/30-12/25 | 1P $40 | 2P/1B $40 | 2P/2B $40 |
| Sun-Thu 8/29-11/29 & Sun-Thu 12/26-5/25 | 1P $54 | 2P/1B $54 | 2P/2B $54 |

XP $10. Check in 4 pm. Reservation deposit required. Comfortable rooms. 18 stories; interior corridors. 709 rooms; 38 suites, $89-99 for up to 2 persons. Pay movies; some safes, coffeemakers, refrigerators. Exercise room. Valet parking. Valet laundry. No pets. Meeting rooms. AE, DI, DS, MC, VI. 3 restaurants; 24-hr coffee shop; $7-29; casino; cocktails; 24-hr room service; entertainment. Ⓓ Ⓢ ⊘ ▦

**GOLD COAST HOTEL** ♦♦♦ Hotel

*1 block W of I-15, exit Flamingo Rd W to 4000 W Flamingo Rd; Box 80750, 89180.*
*(702) 367-7111; (702) 367-8575.*

| Fri-Sat | 1P $75 | 2P/1B $75 | 2P/2B $75 |
| Sun-Thu | 1P $55 | 2P/1B $55 | 2P/2B $55 |

Colonial-Spanish architecture. 10 stories; interior corridors. 711 rooms; 18 beautifully decorated suites with wet bar and refrigerator, $150-300 for 2 persons; luxury-level rooms. Cable TV, free and pay movies; some shower baths; fee for refrigerators, whirlpools. Pool, whirlpool, bowling center, movie theaters. Valet parking. Valet laundry. No pets. Conference facilities. AE, CB, DI, DS, JCB, MC, VI. Dining room; restaurant; 24-hr coffee shop; $5-21; buffet, $7; casino; cocktails and lounge; 24-hr room service; entertainment. Ⓓ Ⓢ ⊘

## GOLDEN NUGGET HOTEL ⒶⒶⒶ      ◆◆◆◆ Hotel
*In the downtown casino center area at 129 E Fremont St; Box 610, 89125.*
*(702) 385-7111; FAX (702) 386-8362.*

| All year | 1P $59-299 | 2P/1B $59-299 | 2P/2B $59-299 |

XP $20. Reservation deposit required. Large rooms, attractive contemporary decor. 10-22 stories; interior corridors. 1907 rooms; 1- and 2-bedroom suites, $275-375 for 2 persons. Cable TV. Pool, whirlpool, video arcade. Fee for health club, massage. Valet parking. Valet laundry. No pets. Conference facilities. AE, DI, DS, MC, VI. 2 dining rooms; restaurant; 24-hr coffee shop; $10-35; buffet, $10; casino; 24-hr room service; cocktails and lounge; entertainment. Ⓓ Ⓢ ⊘ ⓖ ⒵

## HARRAH'S-LAS VEGAS      ◆◆◆ Hotel
*4 mi S on the Strip; 3475 Las Vegas Bl S, 89109.*
*(702) 369-5000; FAX (702) 369-5008.*

| All year | 1P $50-259 | 2P/1B $50-259 | 2P/2B $50-259 |

XP $10; ages 12 and under stay free. Reservation deposit required; 3-day refund notice. 15-35 stories; interior corridors. 2683 rooms; 64 suites, $195-350 for up to 2 persons. Cable TV, free and pay movies; some roll-in showers. Pool, whirlpool; fee for massage, health club. Valet parking. Coin laundry. No pets. Conference facilities. AE, CB, DI, DS, JCB, MC, VI. 4 restaurants; 24-hr coffee shop; $9-40; buffet, $10; cocktails and lounge; entertainment. Ⓓ Ⓢ ⊘ ⓖ ⒵

## HAWTHORN SUITES – LAS VEGAS      Too New To Rate-Suite Motor Inn
*Exit I-15 at E Tropicana Av, ⅓ mi E to Duke Ellington Wy, S to 5051 Duke Ellington Wy, 89119.*
*(702) 739-7000; FAX (702) 739-9350*

| All year [BP] | 1P $85 | 2P/1B $95 | 2P/2B $159 |

Reservation deposit required; 3-day refund notice. Senior discount. 3 stories; exterior corridors, 284 rooms. Cable TV, kitchens. Pool. No pets. AE, DI, DS, MC, VI. Ⓓ Ⓢ ⊘ **(See ad below.)**

## HILTON GRAND VACATIONS CLUB      ◆◆◆ Hotel
*Exit I-15 Flamingo E, N on Strip; directly behind Flamingo Hilton; 3575 Las Vegas Bl S, 89109.*
*(702) 697-2900; FAX (702) 697-2910.*

| All year | 1P $109-199 | 2P/1B $109-199 | 2P/2B $239-399 |

Check in 4 pm. Reservation deposit required; 3-day refund notice. Senior discount. Attractively landscaped grounds and public areas. 17 stories; interior corridors. 291 rooms; 214

2-bedroom units; 146 efficiencies, 145 kitchens. Cable TV, pay movies, VCPs, whirlpools, data ports, roll-in showers. Pool, whirlpool. Valet parking. Valet laundry. No pets. AE, DS, MC, VI. D ⊘

## HOLIDAY INN CASINO BOARDWALK ◆◆◆ Hotel

*I-15 exit Flamingo Bl, S on Strip to 3750 Las Vegas Bl S, 89109.*
*(702) 735-1167; FAX (702) 730-3166*

| | | | |
|---|---|---|---|
| Fri-Sat | 1P $89 | 2P/1B $89 | 2P/2B $89 |
| Sun-Thu | 1P $69 | 2P/1B $69 | 2P/2B $69 |

XP $15. 4-16 stories; interior/exterior corridors. 653 rooms. Cable TV, pay movies; roll-in showers; fee for whirlpools. Pool. No pets. AE, CB, DI, DS, JCB, MC, VI. 2 coffee shops; $7-10. D

## HOLIDAY INN EXPRESS 🆊 ◆◆◆ Motel

*I-15 exit Sahara (#40), 8 mi W to 8669 W Sahara Av, 89117.*
*(702) 256-3766; FAX (702) 256-3763.*

| | | | |
|---|---|---|---|
| All year [CP] | 1P $69-120 | 2P/1B $69-120 | 2P/2B $79-140 |

3 stories; interior corridors. No elevator. 59 rooms; 14 efficiencies, 3 kitchens. Cable TV, movies; some shower baths; fee for microwaves, refrigerators, whirlpools. Heated indoor pool. Coin laundry. Pets. AE, CB, DI, DS, JCB, MC, VI. Restaurants nearby. D S ⊘

## HOWARD JOHNSON HOTEL & CASINO 🆊 ◆◆ Hotel

*Adjacent to I-15, Tropicana W exit; 3111 W Tropicana Av, 89103.*
*(702) 798-1111; FAX (702) 798-7138.*

| | | | |
|---|---|---|---|
| Fri-Sat | 1P $89 | 2P/1B $89 | 2P/2B $89 |
| Sun-Thu | 1P $59 | 2P/1B $59 | 2P/2B $59 |

XP $10; ages 12 and under stay free. Reservation deposit required. Convenient to airport and Strip. 6 stories; interior corridors. 150 rooms. Cable TV, pay movies, rental refrigerators. Pool, whirlpool. Airport transportation. No pets. AE, DI, DS, MC, VI. 24-hr coffee shop; $6-12; cocktails and lounge. D ⊘

## HOWARD JOHNSON INN – AIRPORT ◆ Motel

*Exit I-15, E Tropicana Exit, 1⅛ mi to Paradise Rd, 3/10 mi S to 5100 Paradise Rd, 89119.*
*(702) 798-2777; FAX (702) 736-8295.*

| | | | |
|---|---|---|---|
| Fri-Sat | 1P $65-145 | 2P/1B $65-145 | 2P/2B $65-145 |
| Sun-Thu | 1P $45-125 | 2P/1B $45-125 | 2P/2B $45-125 |

Reservation deposit. Senior discount. 2 stories; exterior corridors. 146 rooms. Cable TV. Pool. Area, Strip and airport transportation. No pets. AE, DI, DS, MC, VI. D ⊘

## LADY LUCK CASINO & HOTEL 🆊 ◆◆ Hotel

*3rd and Ogden; 206 N 3rd St; Box 1060, 89125.*
*(702) 477-3000; FAX (702) 384-2832.*

| | | | |
|---|---|---|---|
| All year | 1P $40-80 | 2P/1B $40-80 | 2P/2B $40-80 |

XP $8. 2-25 stories; interior corridors. 791 rooms; few poolside units; 165 suites with whirlpool bath, $60-100 for 2 persons. Cable TV, pay movies, refrigerators; some whirlpools. Pool. Valet parking. Airport transportation. Valet laundry. No pets. AE, DI, DS, JCB, MC, VI. 2 restaurants; 24-hr coffee shop; $7-24; buffet, $5; casino; 24-hr room service; cocktails and lounge. D S ⊘

## LA QUINTA INN 🆊 ◆◆◆ Motel

*5½ mi S on the Strip; 3782 Las Vegas Bl S, 89109.*
*(702) 739-7457; FAX (702) 736-1129.*

| | | | |
|---|---|---|---|
| Fri-Sat [CP] | 1P $68-77 | 2P/1B $77-86 | 2P/2B $77 |
| Sun-Thu [CP] | 1P $59-68 | 2P/1B $68-77 | 2P/2B $68 |

XP $10; ages 18 and under stay free. Spanish exterior design. 3 stories; exterior corridors. 114 rooms. Cable TV, free and pay movies. Pool. Airport transportation 7 am-10 pm. Small pets only. AE, CB, DI, DS, MC, VI. Coffee shop nearby. D ⊘

## LA QUINTA INN CONVENTION CENTER 🆊 ♦♦♦ Motel
*⅛ mi S of convention center, exit I-15 Flamingo Ave E, ½ mi E of the Strip; 3970 Paradise Rd, 89109.*
*(702) 796-9000; FAX (702) 796-3537.*

| | | | |
|---|---|---|---|
| Fri-Sat [CP] | 1P $78-82 | 2P/1B $78-82 | 2P/2B $78 |
| Sun-Thu [CP] | 1P $68-72 | 2P/1B $68-72 | 2P/2B $68 |

XP $10; ages 18 and under stay free. Large grassy area. 3 stories; interior corridors. 228 rooms; 120 efficiencies, 21 kitchens; some units with balconies, few with patios; 12 1-bedroom units; 9 2-bedroom units; maximum rates for up to 4 persons. Cable TV, pay movies, rental VCPs, safes, whirlpools; some refrigerators, coffeemakers, microwaves. Small pool, whirlpool. Airport and 24-hr Strip transportation. Coin laundry. No pets. Meeting rooms. AE, CB, DI, DS, MC, VI. Coffee shop, 11:30 am-10 pm; $7-14. Ⓓ ⊘

## LAS VEGAS HILTON 🆊 ♦♦♦♦ Hotel
*Exit I-15 at Sahara, 2 mi E, adjacent to convention center; 3000 Paradise Rd; Box 93147, 89193.*
*(702) 732-5111; FAX (702) 732-5805.*

| | | | |
|---|---|---|---|
| All year | 1P $95-275 | 2P/1B $95-275 | 2P/2B $95-275 |

XP $20. Reservation deposit required; 3-day refund notice. 30 stories; interior corridors. 3174 rooms; 300 suites, $310-1250 for up to 2 persons; luxury-level rooms. Cable TV, free and pay movies; some safes, refrigerators, data ports. Pool, whirlpool, 6 lighted tennis courts, putting green, playground, video arcade; fee for health club, massage. Valet parking. Valet laundry. No pets. PCs, secretarial services. Business center, conference facilities, convention oriented. AE, CB, DI, DS, JCB, MC, VI. 8 dining rooms, coffee shop, 24-hr deli; $8-35; buffet, $9-13; cocktails and lounge; 24-hr room service; also Andiamo, see separate listing. Ⓓ Ⓢ ⊘ ♿ ▨

## LAS VEGAS INN TRAVELODGE ♦♦ Motor Inn
*E off I-15, ½ mi W of the Strip, westbound Sahara traffic exit right via Western Av; 1501 W Sahara Av, 89102.*
*(702) 733-0001; FAX (702) 733-1571.*

| | | | |
|---|---|---|---|
| Fri-Sat [CP] | 1P $79-129 | 2P/1B $89-139 | 2P/2B $89-139 |
| Sun-Thu [CP] | 1P $49- 89 | 2P/1B $59- 99 | 2P/2B $59- 99 |

XP $10; ages 12 and under stay free. Senior discount. 3-4 stories; interior corridors. 223 rooms. Cable TV, movies, coffeemakers; some refrigerators. Pool. Airport transportation. Coin laundry. No pets. Meeting rooms. AE, DI, DS, JCB, MC, VI. Coffee shop nearby. Ⓓ ⊘

## LUXOR LAS VEGAS 🆊 ♦♦♦ Resort Hotel
*I-15 exit E Tropicana, just S on the Strip; 3900 Las Vegas Bl S; Box 98640, 89193.*
*(702) 262-4444; FAX (702) 262-4454.*

| | | | |
|---|---|---|---|
| All year | 1P $99-189 | 2P/1B $99-189 | 2P/2B $99-189 |

XP $10. 350-foot glass-faced pyramid, crowned by a 40-billion candlepower vertical light beam. Egyptian decor theme. 30 stories; interior corridors. 4526 rooms; luxury-level rooms. Cable TV, free and pay movies, data ports; some shower baths, whirlpools, roll-in showers. Pool, wading pool, sauna, whirlpools; fee for health club, massage. Special effects attractions, Virtualand arcade, King Tut's Tomb and Museum within atrium. Valet parking. Airport transportation. No pets. AE, CB, DI, DS, JCB, MC, VI. Dining room; 4 restaurants; coffee shop; deli; $10-50; cocktails and lounge; 24-hr room service; entertainment. Ⓓ Ⓢ ⊘ ♿ ▨

## MAIN STREET STATION ♦♦♦ Hotel
*In downtown casino center, 200 N Main St, 89125.*
*(702) 387-1896; FAX (702) 386-4466.*

| | | | |
|---|---|---|---|
| All year | 1P $50-125 | 2P/1B $50-125 | 2P/2B $50-125 |

17 stories; interior corridors. 406 rooms. Cable TV, pay movies; roll-in showers. No pets. AE, CB, DI, DS, MC, VI. Restaurant; 24-hr coffee shop; micro brewery; buffet, $12. Ⓓ Ⓢ ⊘

## MGM GRAND HOTEL CASINO & THEME PARK ♦♦♦ Resort Hotel
*I-15 exit E Tropicana Av; 3799 Las Vegas Bl S, 89109.*
*(702) 891-1111; FAX (702) 891-1030.*

| | | | |
|---|---|---|---|
| All year | 1P $69-259 | 2P/1B $69-259 | 2P/2B $69-259 |

XP $25; ages 12 and under stay free. Reservation deposit required. World's largest hotel; 33-acre magical theme park. 30 stories; interior corridors. 5005 rooms; 400 suites, $169-500 for up to 2 persons. Cable TV, pay movies; some roll-in showers, whirlpools. Heated pool, whirlpool, 5 lighted tennis courts, "King Looey" Youth Center (8 am-midnight), health club, arcade; fee for massage. Valet parking. Valet laundry. No pets. Business center, conference facilities. AE, CB, DI, DS, JCB, MC, VI. 5 restaurants; coffee shop; $10-30; buffet, $10; casino. Ⓓ Ⓢ ⊘ 🚹 🗗

## THE MIRAGE ♦♦♦♦ Resort Hotel
*3½ mi S on the Strip; 3400 Las Vegas Bl S; Box 98544, 89193.*
*(702) 791-7111; FAX (702) 791-7446.*

| | | | |
|---|---|---|---|
| Fri-Sat | 1P $109-399 | 2P/1B $109-399 | 2P/2B $109-399 |
| Sun-Thu | 1P $ 79-399 | 2P/1B $ 79-399 | 2P/2B $ 79-399 |

XP $30. Reservation deposit required. Lavish grounds and unique public areas; home to Siegfried and Roy and their white tigers, also dolphin habitat. Free tram to Treasure Island. 30 stories; interior corridors. 3044 rooms; 1- and 2-bedroom suites, $300-950 for 2 persons; luxury-level rooms. Cable TV, movies, rental VCPs, data ports; some refrigerators, safes, whirlpools, roll-in showers. 2 heated pools, wading pool, whirlpools, putting green, arcade; fee for massage, health club. Valet parking. No pets. PCs, secretarial services. Business center, conference facilities. AE, CB, DI, DS, JCB, MC, VI. Dining room; 6 restaurants; coffee shop; $6-50; buffet $7-13; 24-hr casino; cocktails and lounge; name entertainment. Ⓓ Ⓢ ⊘ 🗗

## MONTE CARLO RESORT & CASINO ♦♦♦ Hotel
*On the Strip between Flamingo Rd & Tropicana Av; 3770 Las Vegas Bl S, 89109.*
*(702) 730-7777; FAX (702) 730-7250.*

| | | | |
|---|---|---|---|
| Fri-Sat | 1P $109-249 | 2P/1B $109-249 | 2P/2B $109-249 |
| Sun-Thu | 1P $ 69-199 | 2P/1B $ 69-199 | 2P/2B $ 69-199 |

XP $15; ages 13 and under stay free. Reservation deposit required; 3-day refund notice. 32 stories; interior corridors. 3014 rooms; luxury-level rooms. Cable TV, pay movies, data ports, roll-in showers; fee for whirlpools. 5 heated pools, whirlpools, saunas, steam rooms, exercise room, 4 lighted tennis courts; fee for massage. Valet parking. Valet laundry. No pets. Business center, conference facilities. AE, DI, DS, MC, VI. 6 restaurants; $8-22; 24-hr room service. Ⓓ Ⓢ ⊘ 🗗

## THE ORLEANS ♦♦♦ Hotel
*Exit I-15 at Tropicana, 1 mi W to 4500 W Tropicana, 89103.*
*(702) 365-7111.*

| | | | |
|---|---|---|---|
| Fri-Sat | 1P $89-109 | 2P/1B $89-109 | 2P/2B $89-109 |
| Sun-Thu | 1P $49- 69 | 2P/1B $49- 69 | 2P/2B $49- 69 |

XP $10. Reservation deposit required. 22 stories. 840 rooms; luxury-level rooms. Cable TV, movies. Pool, whirlpool; fee for bowling. No pets. Conference facilities, meeting rooms. Casino. AE, CB, DI, DS, JCB, MC, VI. 3 restaurants, coffee shop; 24 hrs, $4-20; buffet, $8; 24-hr room service; cocktails and lounge; entertainment. Ⓓ Ⓢ ⊘

## QUALITY INN & KEY LARGO CASINO 🆑 ♦♦ Hotel
*377 E Flamingo Rd, 89109.*
*(702) 733-7777; FAX (702) 369-6911.*

| | | | |
|---|---|---|---|
| Fri-Sat | 1P $75 | 2P/1B $75 | 2P/2B $75 |
| Sun-Thu | 1P $55 | 2P/1B $55 | 2P/2B $55 |

XP $10; ages 18 and under stay free. Attractively landscaped grounds. 3 stories; interior/exterior corridors. 315 rooms. Cable TV, pay movies, coffeemakers, refrigerators; some radios. Heated pool, whirlpool. Area transportation to the Strip. Coin laundry. No pets. Meeting rooms. AE, DI, DS, JCB, MC, VI. Restaurant; 6 am-10 pm; $4-13; cocktails and lounge. ⒟ ▨

### RESIDENCE INN BY MARRIOTT ◆◆◆ Apartment Hotel
*Opposite convention center; 3225 Paradise Rd, 89109.*
*(702) 796-9300; FAX (702) 796-9562.*

| | | | |
|---|---|---|---|
| All year [CP] | 1P $95-319 | 2P/1B $95-319 | 2P/2B $125-329 |

XP $10. Check in 4 pm. Reservation deposit required. 2 stories; exterior corridors. 192 rooms; 48 2-bedroom units. Cable TV, movies, microwaves, kitchens, data ports; some VCPs. Heated pool, whirlpools, sports court. Airport transportation 7 am-10 pm. Coin laundry. Small pets only, $7; $100 deposit. Meeting rooms. AE, CB, DI, DS, JCB, MC, VI. Complimentary snacks and beverages weekdays 5:30-7 pm. ⒟ Ⓢ ∅

### RIO SUITE HOTEL & CASINO ◆◆◆◆ Hotel
*Exit I-15 at Flamingo Rd, ³/₁₀ mi W; 3700 W Flamingo Rd; Box 14160, 89114.*
*(702) 252-7777; FAX (702) 252-8909.*

| | | | |
|---|---|---|---|
| All year | 1P $95-149 | 2P/1B $95-149 | 2P/2B $95-149 |

XP $15. Tropical swim lagoon with white sand, beach and volleyball court. 41 stories; interior corridors. 2563 rooms; specialty suites, $300-850. Cable TV, pay movies, refrigerators, coffeemakers, data ports, safes; some roll-in showers, whirlpools. 2 heated pools, whirlpools, exercise room, video arcade. Fee for massage. Valet parking. Valet laundry. No pets. Fee for PC, secretarial services. Conference facilities. AE, CB, DI, DS, MC, VI. 4 dining rooms; 5 restaurants; coffee shop; 24-hr deli; $8-45; seafood buffet, $17; international buffet, $9; casino; cocktails; entertainment. ⒟ Ⓢ ∅ 🔲 ▨

### RIVIERA HOTEL ◆◆ Hotel
*From I-15, exit E Sahara; 2901 Las Vegas Bl S, 89109.*
*(702) 734-5110; FAX (702) 794-9451.*

| | | | |
|---|---|---|---|
| All year | 1P $59-145 | 2P/1B $59-145 | 2P/2B $59-145 |

XP $20. Reservation deposit required. Wedding chapel. 24 stories; interior corridors. 2073 rooms; many large rooms. Cable TV, pay movies, safes; some radios, refrigerators. Pool, whirlpool, 2 lighted tennis courts. Fee for health club, massage. Valet parking. Valet laundry. No pets. Secretarial services. Business center, conference facilities, convention oriented. AE, CB, DI, DS, JCB, MC, VI. 3 restaurants; 24-hr coffee shop; $8-35; buffet, $6-9 in casino; cocktails and lounge; entertainment. ⒟ Ⓢ ∅ ▨

### ST. TROPEZ ALL SUITE HOTEL ⒶⒶ ◆◆◆ Complex
*2 mi S of convention center at Paradise Rd; 455 E Harmon Av, 89109.*
*(702) 369-5400; FAX (702) 369-1150.*

| | | | |
|---|---|---|---|
| All year [CP] | 1P $95-200 | 2P/1B $95-200 | 2P/2B $120-200 |

XP $12; ages 18 and under stay free. Surrounding attractively landscaped grounds. 2 stories; interior/exterior corridors. 149 rooms; courtyard units with patio or deck; whirlpool units, $120-160 for up to 2 persons. Cable TV, pay movies, coffeemakers, VCPs, honor bars, safes; some shower baths, roll-in showers, whirlpools. Pool, whirlpool, exercise room. Area transportation to the Strip and airport. No pets. Meeting rooms. AE, DI, DS, MC, VI. Complimentary evening beverages. Cocktail lounge; restaurant nearby. ⒟ ∅ ▨

### SAM'S TOWN HOTEL ◆◆◆ Hotel
*1 mi E of I-515 and SR 93/95, Flamingo exit; 5111 Boulder Hwy, 89122.*
*(702) 456-7777; FAX (702) 454-8014.*

| | | | |
|---|---|---|---|
| Fri-Sat | 1P $75-100 | 2P/1B $75-155 | 2P/2B $75-155 |
| Sun-Thu | 1P $50- 65 | 2P/1B $50- 80 | 2P/2B $50- 80 |

XP $5; ages 12 and under stay free. Reservation deposit required. Central indoor park with waterfall; nightly laser and water show. Southwestern decor. 9 stories; interior corridors. 650 rooms. Cable TV, pay movies; some microwaves, refrigerators, whirlpools, roll-in showers. Pool, whirlpool; fee for bowling, sand volleyball, video arcade. Valet parking. Area and airport transportation. No pets. Conference facilities. AE, CB, DI, DS, MC, VI. 6 restaurants; coffee shop; deli; $6-18; 24-hr buffet, $9; casino; cocktails and lounge; 24-hr room service; entertainment. Ⓓ Ⓢ Ⓧ

### SILVERTON HOTEL & CASINO ⒶⒶ                                      ♦♦ Hotel
*Formerly Boomtown Hotel-Casino. I-15 exit 33 W to 3333 Blue Diamond Rd, 89139.*
*(702) 263-7777; FAX (702) 896-5635.*

| | | | |
|---|---|---|---|
| Fri-Sat | 1P $70 | 2P/1B $70 | 2P/2B $70 |
| Sun-Thu | 1P $49 | 2P/1B $49 | 2P/2B $49 |

XP $5. Replica of an 1800s Old West frontier mining town. 5 stories; interior corridors. 300 rooms; 12 suites with whirlpool, $150-195 for up to 2 persons. Cable TV, coffeemakers. Heated pool, wading pool, whirlpool. Fee for child care. Area transportation to the Strip. Valet laundry. No pets. Meeting rooms. AE, CB, DI, DS, MC, VI. 24-hr coffee shop; buffet $7, in casino $6-18; cocktails; entertainment. Ⓓ Ⓢ Ⓧ

### SOMERSET HOUSE MOTEL ⒶⒶ                                      ♦♦ Motel
*3 mi S, 1 block E off the Strip. 1 block from convention center; 294 Convention Center Dr, 89109.*
*(702) 735-4411; FAX (702) 369-2388.*

| | | | |
|---|---|---|---|
| Fri-Sat | 1P $40 | 2P/1B $50 | 2P/2B $50 |
| Sun-Thu | 1P $32 | 2P/1B $40 | 2P/2B $40 |

XP $5; discount for ages 12 and under. Reservation deposit required; 3-day refund notice. Weekly rates available. Senior discount. 3 stories; interior/exterior corridors. 104 rooms; 17 efficiencies, 63 kitchens. Movies, refrigerators; some shower baths, roll-in showers, balconies. Pool. Coin laundry. No pets. AE, CB, DI, MC, VI. Ⓓ Ⓧ Ⓖ

### TEXAS STATION GAMBLING HALL & HOTEL                          ♦♦♦ Motor Inn
*On Business US 95, 3 mi N of downtown at 2101 Texas Star Ln, 89030.*
*(702) 631-1000; FAX (702) 631-8120.*

| | | | |
|---|---|---|---|
| Fri-Sat | 1P $89-129 | 2P/1B $89-129 | 2P/2B $89-129 |
| Sun-Thu | 1P $49- 99 | 2P/1B $49- 99 | 2P/2B $49- 99 |

Reservation deposit required. 6 stories; interior corridors. 200 rooms. Cable TV. Pool. No pets. AE, CB, DI, DS, MC, VI. Restaurant; coffee shop; $9-18. Ⓓ Ⓢ Ⓧ

### TREASURE ISLAND AT THE MIRAGE                                ♦♦♦ Resort Hotel
*3½ mi S on the Strip; 3300 Las Vegas Bl S; Box 7711, 89193.*
*(702) 894-7111; FAX (702) 894-7414.*

| | | | |
|---|---|---|---|
| Fri-Sat | 1P $99-299 | 2P/1B $99-299 | 2P/2B $99-299 |
| Sun-Thu | 1P $59-299 | 2P/1B $59-299 | 2P/2B $59-299 |

XP $25. Reservation deposit required. Pirate-themed resort; home to Cirque du Soleil. 36 stories; interior corridors. 2891 rooms; 212 1-bedroom suites, $100-500 for up to 2 persons. Pay movies, data ports; some whirlpools. Pool, whirlpool, wading pool, water slide, arcade; fee for massage, health club. Area transportation to The Mirage. Valet parking. Valet laundry. No pets. Secretarial services; fee for PC. Conference facilities, business center. AE, CB, DI, DS, JCB, MC, VI. 2 dining rooms; 4 restaurants; coffee shop; $8-30; 3 theme buffets, $5-9; casino; cocktails and lounge; Mystère show, extra charge; entertainment. Ⓓ Ⓢ Ⓧ Ⓖ Ⓩ

# Restaurants

### ANDIAMO ⒶⒶ                                                   ♦♦♦ Regional Italian
*In Las Vegas Hilton; 3000 Paradise Rd, 89109.*
*(702) 732-5111.*
Dinner $20-30. Open 6-11 pm. Reservations suggested. Valet parking. Casual attire.

Comfortable and elegant surroundings; nice variety of dishes. A la carte. Cocktails and lounge. AE, CB, DI, MC, VI. ⊘

### ANDRE'S FRENCH RESTAURANT       ♦♦♦ French
*At Lewis St and 401 S 6th St, 89101.*
*(702) 385-5016.*
Dinner $20-44. Open 6-11 pm. Closed major holidays. Reservations suggested. Valet parking. Semiformal attire. Country-French decor; several dining rooms. Health-conscious menu items, a la carte. Cocktails and lounge. AE, CB, DI, JCB, MC, VI. ⊘

### ANTHONY'S FINE DINING       ♦♦♦ Continental
*Exit I-15 at Tropicana; E 3 mi to 1550 E Tropicana Av, 89119.*
*(702) 795-6000.*
Lunch $6-25, dinner $13-24. Open Sun-Fri 11 am-11 pm, Sat 5-11 pm. Closed 1/1, 12/25. Reservations suggested. Casual attire. Casual elegance with an Italian flair. Children's menu, early bird specials, a la carte. Cocktails. AE, DI, MC, VI. ⊘

### BATTISTA'S HOLE IN THE WALL       ♦ Italian
*I-15 exit Flamingo Rd E ³⁄₁₀ mi, 1 block E of the Strip; 4041 Audrie, 89109.*
*(702) 732-1424.*
Dinner $16-30. Open 5-10:30 pm, Sat to 11 pm. Closed Thanksgiving, 12/25. Reservations suggested. Casual attire. Rustic decor. Dinners include house wine and cappuccino. Cocktails and lounge. AE, CB, DI, MC, VI. ⊘

### COUNTRY INN       ♦♦ American
*2 mi E of the Strip; 2425 E Desert Inn Rd, 89121.*
*(702) 731-5035.*
Lunch and dinner $6-15. Open 7 am-10 pm; Fri and Sat to 11 pm. Closed 12/25. Casual attire. Attractive country decor; casual atmosphere. Children's menu, a la carte. Beer and wine only. AE, CB, DI, DS, MC, VI. ⊘

### COUNTRY INN       ♦♦ American
*Exit I-15 Charleston, 4 mi W, S on Rainbow ³⁄₁₀ mi; 1401 S Rainbow, 89102.*
*(702) 254-0520.*
Lunch $4-6, dinner $4-15. Open 7 am-10 pm; Fri and Sat to 11 pm. Closed 12/25. Reservations suggested. Casual attire. Attractive country decor, traditional dishes and friendly atmosphere. Children's menu, a la carte. Beer and wine only. AE, CB, DI, DS, MC, VI. X

### GOLDEN STEER       ♦♦ Steakhouse
*Exit I-15 at Sahara, ³⁄₁₀ mi E, 1 block W of the Strip; 308 W Sahara Av, 89102.*
*(702) 384-4470.*
Dinner $25-40. Open 5-11:30 pm. Closed Thanksgiving and 12/25. Reservations suggested. Valet parking. Semiformal attire. Quiet atmosphere. Varied menu; chicken, veal and seafood. Italian specialties. A la carte. Cocktails and lounge. AE, CB, DI, MC, VI. ⊘

### KIEFER'S ATOP THE CARRIAGE HOUSE       ♦♦♦ Continental
*105 E Harmon, 89119.*
*(702) 739-8000.*
Dinner $15-30. Open 7 am-10 and 5-10 pm; Fri and Sat to midnight. Reservations suggested. Casual attire. Views of city, very romantic atmosphere. A la carte. Cocktails and lounge. AE, CB, DI, DS, MC, VI. ⊘

### MONTE CARLO RESTAURANT   ⚇      ♦♦♦♦ French
*On the Strip; I-15 NB exit E Flamingo Av, SB exit E Sahara Av; in Desert Inn at 3145 Las Vegas Bl S, 89109.*
*(702) 733-4444.*
Dinner $65-85. Open 6-11 pm. Closed Tue & Wed. Reservations suggested. Valet parking.

Semiformal attire. Long-established, service-oriented dining room, very intimate atmosphere. World class food and service. A la carte, Sun brunch. Cocktails. AE, CB, DI, DS, MC, VI. Smoke-free premises. ⊘

**PHILIPS SUPPER HOUSE**  ♦♦♦ **American**
*2⅓ mi W of the Strip between Arville St and Decatur Bl; 4545 W Sahara Av, 89102.*
*(702) 873-5222.*
Dinner $15-32. Open 4:30-11 pm. Reservations suggested. Casual attire. Prime eastern beef, seafood and Italian specialties. Early bird specials. Cocktails and lounge. AE, CB, DI, DS, MC, VI. ⊘

**YOLIE'S BRAZILIAN STEAK HOUSE**  ♦♦ **Brazilian**
*On upper level of Citibank Park Plaza; 3900 Paradise Rd, Ste Z, 89109.*
*(702) 794-0700.*
Lunch $7-13, dinner $15-44. Open 11:30 am-11 pm; Sat and Sun from 5 pm. Reservations suggested. Casual attire. Informal atmosphere. Variety of meats served from a skewer; also lamb, chicken and fish specialties. Children's menu, a la carte. Cocktails and lounge. Entertainment. AE, CB, DI, DS, MC, VI. ⊘

# Laughlin

## Lodging

**AVI HOTEL & CASINO**  Ⓐ  ♦♦♦ **Hotel**
*9 mi N on Needles Hwy or Casino Dr; from I-40 exit W Broadway, 12 mi N at 10000 Aha Macav Pkwy; Box 77011, 89028-7011.*
*(702) 535-5555; FAX (702) 535-5400.*

| | | | |
|---|---|---|---|
| Fri-Sat | 1P $45-99 | 2P/1B $45-99 | 2P/2B $45-99 |
| Sun-Thu | 1P $20-55 | 2P/1B $20-55 | 2P/2B $20-55 |

4 stories; interior corridors. 300 rooms. Cable TV, pay movies; fee for refrigerators, whirlpools. Pool, whirlpool, beach, swimming, marina, boat ramp; rental boats; fee for wave runners. Valet laundry. No pets. Conference facilities. AE, DS, MC, VI. Dining room, coffee shop & deli; 24 hrs; $10-20; casino buffet, $6-8; cocktails and lounge; entertainment. Ⓓ Ⓢ ⊘

**BAYSHORE INN**  ♦ **Motel**
*7 mi S of Davis Dam; 1955 W Casino Dr; Box 31377, 89029.*
*(702) 299-9010; FAX (702) 299-9194.*

| | | | |
|---|---|---|---|
| Fri-Sat | 1P ... | 2P/1B $55 | 2P/2B $55 |
| Sun-Thu | 1P $25 | 2P/1B $25 | 2P/2B $25 |

Maximum rates for up to 4 persons. Central pool deck. 3 stories; interior corridors. 87 rooms. Cable TV. Small pool, whirlpool. Small pets only, $10. DS, MC, VI. Cocktails and lounge. Restaurant nearby. Ⓓ Ⓢ ⊘

**COLORADO BELLE HOTEL & CASINO**  ♦♦ **Hotel**
*3 mi S of Davis Dam; 2100 S Casino Dr; Box 77000, 89028.*
*(702) 298-4000; FAX (702) 299-0669.*

| | | | |
|---|---|---|---|
| Fri-Sat | 1P $45-60 | 2P/1B $45-60 | 2P/2B $45-60 |
| Sun-Thu | 1P $21-39 | 2P/1B $39 | 2P/2B $39 |

Maximum rates for up to 4 persons. On the Colorado River, riverboat design. 6 stories; interior/exterior corridors. 1230 rooms. Cable TV, shower baths, pay movies; some refrigerators, roll-in showers; fee for safes. 2 pools, whirlpool. Valet parking. No pets. Meeting rooms. AE, CB, DI, DS, MC, VI. 3 restaurants; coffee shop; $9-30; buffet, $5; cocktails and lounge; entertainment. Ⓓ Ⓢ ⊘ ⑦

## DON LAUGHLIN'S RIVERSIDE RESORT HOTEL & CASINO  ♦♦♦ Hotel
*2 mi S of Davis Dam, across river from Bullhead City, AZ; 1650 S Casino Wy, 89029.*
*(702) 298-2535; FAX (702) 298-2614.*

| | | | |
|---|---|---|---|
| Fri-Sat | 1P $49-91 | 2P/1B $49-91 | 2P/2B $49-91 |
| Sun-Thu | 1P $25-71 | 2P/1B $25-71 | 2P/2B $25-71 |

Maximum rates for up to 4 persons. On the Colorado River. 26 stories; interior corridors. 1403 rooms. Cable TV, pay movies; some shower baths, roll-in showers; fee for refrigerators, whirlpools. 2 pools, arcade, 6 movie theaters. Valet parking. Pets, $8; $100 deposit. Meeting rooms. AE, CB, DI, DS, MC, VI. 2 dining rooms; restaurant; 24-hr coffee shop; casino; $7-30; buffet, $6; cocktails; name entertainment. D S ∅ ⧄

## EDGEWATER HOTEL & CASINO  ⬤  ♦♦♦ Hotel
*2³/₁₀ mi S of Davis Dam; 2020 S Casino Dr; Box 77000, 89028.*
*(702) 298-2453; FAX (702) 298-8165.*

| | | | |
|---|---|---|---|
| Fri-Sat | 1P $40-65 | 2P/1B $40-65 | 2P/2B $40-65 |
| Sun-Thu | 1P $21-38 | 2P/1B $21-38 | 2P/2B $21-38 |

Maximum rates for up to 4 persons. Reservation deposit required; cancellation fee. Senior discount. Southwestern decor. American Indian art. 3-26 stories; interior corridors. 1450 rooms. Cable TV, pay movies; some refrigerators, shower baths, roll-in showers. Pool, whirlpool, arcade. Valet parking. Valet laundry. No pets. AE, CB, DI, DS, MC, VI. Dining room; 2 restaurants; coffee shop; deli; $7-25; 24-hr buffet, $5; cocktails and lounge; entertainment. D S ∅ ⧄

## FLAMINGO HILTON LAUGHLIN  ♦♦♦ Hotel
*2 mi S of Davis Dam; 1900 S Casino Dr, 89029.*
*(702) 298-5111; FAX (702) 298-5129.*

| | | | |
|---|---|---|---|
| Fri-Sat | 1P $55 | 2P/1B $55 | 2P/2B $55 |
| Sun-Thu | 1P $25 | 2P/1B $25 | 2P/2B $25 |

XP $9; ages 18 and under stay free. Most rooms view Colorado River. Spacious rooms. 18 stories; interior corridors. 1972 rooms; suites $275-325 for up to 5 persons. Cable TV, pay movies, data ports; some radios; fee for refrigerators. Pool, 3 lighted tennis courts, massage. Valet laundry. No pets. Conference facilities, meeting rooms. AE, CB, DI, DS, JCB, MC, VI. 2 restaurants, coffee shop; 24 hrs; $9-21; buffet, $7; casino; cocktails and lounge; entertainment. D S ∅ ⬠ ⧄

## GOLDEN NUGGET LAUGHLIN  ♦♦♦ Hotel
*3¹/₈ mi S of Davis Dam; 2300 S Casino Dr; Box 77111, 89028.*
*(702) 298-7111; FAX (702) 298-7122.*

| | | | |
|---|---|---|---|
| All year | 1P $21-65 | 2P/1B $21-65 | 2P/2B $21-65 |

XP $7. 30-foot glass-topped atrium with more than 500 tropical flora from around the world; tropical motif throughout. 4 stories; interior corridors. 300 rooms; 4 suites, $150 for up to 2 persons. Cable TV; some shower baths, roll-in showers. Pool, whirlpool, arcade. Valet parking. Valet laundry. No pets. AE, DS, MC, VI. Restaurant; coffee shop, 24 hrs; $5-10; buffet, $5; casino; cocktail and lounge. D S ∅ ⧄

## HARRAH'S CASINO HOTEL  ♦♦♦ Hotel
*5 mi S of Davis Dam, on the river; 2900 S Casino Dr, 89029.*
*(702) 298-4600; FAX (702) 298-6896.*

| | | | |
|---|---|---|---|
| Fri-Sat | 1P $25-180 | 2P/1B $25-180 | 2P/2B $25-180 |
| Sun-Thu | 1P $25-140 | 2P/1B $25-140 | 2P/2B $25-140 |

XP $5. Reservation deposit required; 3-day refund notice. Southwest architecture. On the Colorado River. 20 stories; exterior corridors. 1657 rooms. Cable TV, pay movies; some shower baths, refrigerators. 2 pools, whirlpools, beach, video game room; fee for massage, health club. Valet parking. Valet laundry. No pets. Conference facilities, secretarial services. AE, CB, DI, DS, MC, VI. Dining room, restaurant, coffee shop; $10-25; cocktails and lounge; also William Fisk's Steakhouse, see separate listing. D S ∅

**RAMADA EXPRESS HOTEL & CASINO**   &#9650;&#9650;&#9650; Hotel
*3 mi S of Davis Dam; 2121 S Casino Dr; Box 77771, 89028.*
*(702) 298-4200; FAX (702) 298-4619.*

| | | | |
|---|---|---|---|
| Fri-Sat | 1P $54-89 | 2P/1B $54-89 | 2P/2B $54-89 |
| Sun-Thu | 1P $23-34 | 2P/1B $23-34 | 2P/2B $23-34 |

XP $5; ages 18 and under stay free. Turn-of-the-century railroad motif. 12-23 stories; interior corridors. 1500 rooms. Pay movies; some honor bars, coffeemakers, radios, refrigerators, shower baths, roll-in showers. Pool, whirlpool, wading pool, video arcade, train ride. Valet parking. Valet laundry. No pets. AE, CB, DI, DS, MC, VI. 3 restaurants; coffee shop; deli, 24 hrs; $8-27; buffet, $5; casino; cocktail lounge. Ⓓ Ⓢ ⊘ 🚗

## Restaurant

**WILLIAM FISK'S STEAKHOUSE**   &#9670;&#9670; American
*In Harrah's Casino Hotel; 2900 S Casino Dr, 89029.*
*(702) 298-6832.*
Dinner $15-25. Open 5-10 pm; Fri and Sat to 11 pm. Reservations suggested. Valet parking. Semiformal attire. Intimate dining atmosphere overlooking Colorado River. A la carte. Cocktails. AE, DI, DS, MC, VI. ⊘

# Primm

## Lodging

**PRIMADONNA RESORT & CASINO**   &#9670;&#9670; Motor Inn
*45 mi S of Las Vegas, E of and adjacent to I-15; Primm exit; Box 19119, Las Vegas 89019.*
*(702) 382-1212; FAX (702) 874-5195.*

| | | | |
|---|---|---|---|
| Fri-Sat | 1P $49 | 2P/1B $49 | 2P/2B $49 |
| Sun-Thu | 1P $29 | 2P/1B $29 | 2P/2B $29 |

XP $5; ages 12 and under stay free. 2-night minimum stay Fri and Sat. 4 stories; interior corridors. 660 rooms. Cable TV, pay movies, coffeemakers; some shower baths, roll-in showers; fee for refrigerators, whirlpools. Pool (seasonal), whirlpool, putting green, video game room, playground, Ferris wheel, carousel, bowling center, monorail; fee for 18-holes golf. Valet parking. No pets. Conference facilities. AE, DI, DS, MC, VI. Restaurant; coffee shop; $5-14; 24-hr buffet, $4-5; cocktails and lounge. Ⓓ Ⓢ ⊘ ♿ 🚗

**WHISKEY PETE'S HOTEL & CASINO**   &#9670;&#9670; Hotel
*45 mi S of Las Vegas, W of and adjacent to I-15; Primm exit; Box 19119, Las Vegas 89019.*
*(702) 382-4388; FAX (702) 679-6606.*

| | | | |
|---|---|---|---|
| Fri-Sat | 1P $49 | 2P/1B $49 | 2P/2B $49 |
| Sun-Thu | 1P $25 | 2P/1B $25 | 2P/2B $25 |

XP $5; ages 12 and under stay free. 2-night minimum stay Fri and Sat. Reservation deposit required. 2-19 stories; interior corridors. 777 rooms; suites, $75-200 for 2 persons. Pay movies, coffeemakers; fee for whirlpools. Pool, whirlpool, water slide; fee for 18-holes golf. Valet parking. No pets. Conference facilities. AE, CB, DI, DS, MC, VI. Dining room; coffee shop, 24 hrs; $5-25; buffet, $5; casino; cocktails; entertainment. Ⓓ Ⓢ ⊘

# Bullhead City, Arizona

## Lodging

**BEST WESTERN BULLHEAD CITY INN**   &#9670;&#9670;&#9670; Motel
*1½ mi S of Laughlin Bridge on SR 95, then just E to 2360 4th St, 86429.*
*(520) 754-3000; FAX (520) 754-5234.*

| | | | |
|---|---|---|---|
| All year [CP] | 1P $36 | 2P/1B $40 | 2P/2B $40 |

XP $5; ages 17 and under stay free. Reservation deposit required. Weekly and monthly rates available. Pool at center of property. Rooms decorated in light, contemporary colors. 2 stories;

exterior corridors. 88 rooms. Cable TV, movies, refrigerators; some microwaves. Pool, whirlpool. Pets, $5; $25 deposit. AE, CB, DI, DS, JCB, MC, VI. Ⓓ Ⓢ ⊘

### DAYS INN ♦♦ Motel
*3½ mi S of Laughlin Bridge on SR 95, then just E; 2200 Karis Dr, 86442.*
*(520) 758-1711; FAX (520) 758-7937.*

| | | | |
|---|---|---|---|
| All year [CP] | 1P $58 | 2P/1B $58 | 2P/2B $58 |

XP $5; ages 12 and under stay free. Rooms are decorated in light colors. 3 stories; interior corridors. 68 rooms; 7 1-bedroom suites, $53 for 2 persons. Cable TV, movies, rental VCPs, refrigerators; some shower baths, microwaves, no utensils. Pool, whirlpool. Coin laundry. Small pets only, $10; $50 deposit. AE, CB, DI, DS, JCB, MC, VI. Ⓓ Ⓢ ⊘

### ECONO LODGE RIVERSIDE ⒶⒶⒶ ♦♦ Motel
*3½ mi S of Laughlin Bridge on SR 95; 1717 Hwy 95, 86442.*
*(520) 758-8080; FAX (520) 758-8283.*

| | | | |
|---|---|---|---|
| Fri-Sat [CP] | 1P $36 | 2P/1B $45 | 2P/2B $59 |
| Sun-Thu [CP] | 1P $26 | 2P/1B $26 | 2P/2B $35 |

Sun-Thu XP $6; ages 12 and under stay free. At the Colorado River; contemporary-style rooms decorated in light colors. 2 stories; exterior corridors. 64 rooms; 13 riverfront suites with microwave, refrigerator and balcony, $59-95 for 2 persons. Cable TV; some shower baths, refrigerators, microwaves. Heated pool. Coin laundry. No pets. AE, DS, MC, VI. Ⓓ Ⓢ ⊘

### LAKE MOHAVE RESORT ⒶⒶⒶ ♦ Resort Motor Inn
*In the Lake Mead National Recreation Area at Katherine Landing, 3 mi N of SR 68 and Davis Dam, 86430.*
*(520) 754-3245; FAX (520) 754-1125.*

| | | | |
|---|---|---|---|
| All year | 1P $60-69 | 2P/1B $60-69 | 2P/2B $73-83 |

XP $6. Rooms furnished in Western theme. 2 stories; exterior corridors. 51 rooms; 14 efficiencies. Some shower baths. Beach, swimming, water-skiing, fishing. Boat ramp, marina, rental boats, houseboats. Coin laundry. Pets, $25 deposit. DS, MC, VI. Restaurant at Lake Mohave across from establishment, 8 am-8 pm; Fri and Sat from 7 am; $9-14; cocktails. Ⓓ

### MOTEL 6-1116 ⒶⒶⒶ ♦ Motel
*3 mi S of Laughlin Bridge; 1616 SR 95, 86442.*
*(520) 763-1002; FAX (520) 763-3868.*

| | | | |
|---|---|---|---|
| All year | 1P $23-29 | 2P/1B $28-35 | 2P/2B $28-35 |

XP $3; ages 17 and under stay free. 2 stories; interior corridors. 118 rooms. Cable TV, movies; some shower baths. Heated pool. Small pets only. AE, CB, DI, DS, JCB, MC, VI. Ⓓ ☒

### SUNRIDGE HOTEL & CONFERENCE CENTER ⒶⒶⒶ ♦♦♦ Motor Inn
*3 mi N on SR 95, 1¹⁄₁₀ mi E on SR 68 in Sunridge Estates; 839 Landon Dr, 86429.*
*(520) 754-4700; FAX (520) 754-1225.*

| | | | |
|---|---|---|---|
| Fri-Sat [CP] | 1P $59 | 2P/1B $59 | 2P/2B $59 |
| Sun-Thu [CP] | 1P $49 | 2P/1B $49 | 2P/2B $49 |

XP $5; ages 18 and under stay free. Weekly and monthly rates available. On quiet hillside off highway. 4 stories; exterior corridors. 154 rooms. Cable TV; some refrigerators. Heated pool, whirlpool, exercise room. Coin laundry. Small pets only, $50 deposit. Conference facilities. AE, CB, DI, DS, MC, VI. Restaurant, 7-10 am and 5-9 pm; $5-11; cocktails. Ⓓ Ⓢ ⊘

# Restaurant

### TOWNE'S SQUARE CAFE ♦♦ American
*3⅖ mi S of Laughlin Bridge on SR 95, 1751 W Hwy 95, Ste 25, 86442.*
*(520) 763-2477.*

Lunch $5-7; dinner $7-16. Open 5:30 am-10:30 pm; Fri and Sat to midnight. Casual attire. Nice family-style restaurant with homey decor and atmosphere. Good selection of sandwiches, beef, chicken and seafood entrees. Children's menu, seniors' menu, health-conscious menu, carryout. Beer and wine only. AE, DI, DS, MC, VI. ⊘

# Campgrounds & Trailer Parks

*Warm weather and nearby scenic and recreation areas attract thousands of campers to Las Vegas and Laughlin every year. Camping accommodations range from simple RV lots located close to the gambling action and glitz to more rugged settings in surrounding areas, including Bullhead City, Arizona. The campgrounds in this section are listed alphabetically by city or closest recreation area—**Boulder City**, **Lake Mead National Recreation Area (Lake Mead** and **Lake Mohave)**, **Las Vegas**, **Primm**, **Red Rock Canyon National Conservation Area**, **Spring Mountains National Recreation Area**, **Valley of Fire State Park** and **Bullhead City**, **Arizona**. Unless otherwise noted, campgrounds are open all year.*

*I*n the following listings, fees shown are for one night's camping—usually for two people—and unless specified, include a recreational vehicle or automobile (with or without a trailer). Electricity, water and sewer RV hookups are indicated by the letters **E**, **W** and **S**, respectively. **El** indicates elevation in feet.

Campgrounds marked with a √ have been inspected by Auto Club representatives and meet AAA requirements for recommendation. The campgrounds without the check mark are publicly operated facilities that may not meet all AAA standards for approval, but are listed here as a convenience for travelers. Privately operated campgrounds not meeting AAA requirements are not listed. The ⓐ in a listing identifies an establishment as a AAA Official Appointment; it indicates that the campground has expressed a particular interest in serving AAA members.

The administering agency for each campground is shown at the end of the individual listings, i.e., National Forest (NF); National Park Service (NPS); County; State; Bureau of Land Management (BLM); and Private.

Bringing the family pet? Pets are welcome in most campgrounds. Be aware that some campgrounds charge a nominal fee for pets (these are noted).

RV towing and tire-change service is available to AAA members for motor homes, campers and travel/camping trailers. Members should contact their local Auto Club for further details.

## Reservations

Campsites that can be reserved by phoning the campground or administering agency directly indicate "reservations" or "reservation deposit required." Any other reservation system is outlined; otherwise, it's "first come, first served."

Reservations for some national forest campgrounds can be made by calling the **National Forest Reservation Center** at (800) 280-2267 or TTD (800) 879-4496 (for the hearing/speech impaired). National Forest sites can be reserved up to 240 days prior to arrival; cancellation notice is 13 days or less for family sites and 29 days or less for group sites. Discover, MasterCard and VISA cards are accepted. There is a nonrefundable reservation fee of $8.65 for one family campsite, $17.35 for one group site. The cancellation fee is $8.65, plus additional penalties for no-show or late cancellations. The reservation center is open from January through March, Monday through Friday 9 a.m. to 9 p.m.; April through September, hours Monday through Friday are 9 a.m. to 11 p.m., Saturday and Sunday 9 a.m. to 7 p.m.; from October through December, the center is open Monday through Friday from 11 a.m. to 7 p.m. Hours listed are for Eastern Time and are subject to change.

Major credit cards honored by camp-grounds appear at the end of each applic-able listing and are abbreviated as follows:

| | |
|---|---|
| AE | American Express |
| CB | Carte Blanche |
| DI | Diners Club International |
| DS | Discover |
| MC | MasterCard |
| VI | VISA |

**All camping fees are subject to change.**

# Boulder City

**BOULDER OAKS RV RESORT** √
*1010 Industrial Rd, 89005.*
*(702) 294-4425; FAX (702) 294-4426.*
$20-28 per night. Reservation deposit required. Some sites with view of distant Lake Mead. 275 RV sites. 275 EWS. 50 amps. Disposal station. Cable TV and phone hookups. Heated pool, sauna. Groceries. Laundry. Pets. AE, CB, DI, MC, VI. (Private)

# Lake Mead National Recreation Area

**HEADQUARTERS** *25 mi SE of Las Vegas; c/o 601 Nevada Hwy, Boulder City 89005. (702) 293-8990, 293-8906.*

## Lake Mead

**BOULDER BEACH** √
*6 mi NE of Boulder City on SR 166, 89005.*
*(702) 293-8906.*
$10 per night. 30-day stay limit. Reservations not accepted. 146 tent/RV sites. Flush toilets. Rental boats; boat ramp. Groceries. Coin laundry. Pets. (NPS)

**CALLVILLE BAY** √
*22 mi NE of Henderson on SR 147/167, 89015.*
*(702) 293-8906.*
$10 per night. 90-day stay limit. Reservations not accepted. 80 tent/RV sites. Flush toilets, no showers. Rental boats; boat ramp. Coin laundry. Pets. (NPS)

**ECHO BAY** √
*30 mi S of Overton on SR 167, 89005.*
*(702) 293-8906.*
$10 per night. 90-day stay limit. Reservations not accepted. 153 tent/RV sites. Flush toilets, no showers. Rental boats; boat ramp. Coin laundry. Pets. (NPS)

**LAS VEGAS BAY** √
*8 mi NE of Henderson or 13 mi NW of Boulder City on SR 166, 89005.*
*(702) 293-8906.*
$10 per night. 30-day stay limit. Reservations not accepted. 89 tent/RV sites. Flush toilets, no showers. Rental boats; boat ramp. Pets. (NPS)

**TEMPLE BAR** √
*26 mi N of US 93 on Temple Bar Rd.*
*(702) 293-8906.*
$10 per night. 30-day stay limit. Reservations not accepted. 152 tent/RV sites. Disposal station. Flush toilets, no showers. Boats; boat ramp. Groceries. Coin laundry. Pets. (NPS)

# Lake Mohave

### COTTONWOOD COVE √
*14 mi E of Searchlight on SR 164; Box 123, Searchlight 89046.*
*(702) 293-8906.*
$10 per night. 90-day stay limit. 145 tent/RV sites. 75 EWS. Flush toilets. Rental boats; boat ramp. Groceries. Coin laundry. Pets. (NPS)

### COTTONWOOD COVE RV PARK & MARINA ⓦ √
*Between Las Vegas and Needles; 14 mi E of Searchlight, off US 95 at Lake Mohave; Box 1000, 89046.*
*(702) 297-1464.*
$17 per night for 8 persons. Credit card guarantee required; 5-day refund notice. Desert landscape. 73 RV sites. 73 EWS. Disposal station, piped water, flush toilets, coin-operated showers. Air conditioning, $3. Beach, swimming, fishing; boat ramp, marina. Fee for houseboats, powerboats, water-skiing and equipment. Snack bar; groceries, propane. Coin laundry. Pets. AE, DS, MC, VI. (Private)

### KATHERINE LANDING √
*5 mi N of Bullhead City, off US 95/SR 68; 601 Nevada Hwy, Boulder City, NV 89005.*
*(520) 754-3272.*
$10 per night. 14-day stay limit. 172 tent/RV sites. Disposal station, flush toilets, piped water. Rental boats; boat ramp; fishing, swimming. Coin laundry. Pets. (NPS)

# Las Vegas

### BOOMTOWN RV RESORT ⓦ √
*From I-15, exit W Blue Diamond Rd (exit 33) to 3333 Blue Diamond Rd, 89139.*
*(702) 263-7777; FAX (702) 897-4208.*
Fri-Sat: $20 per night; Sun-Thu: $18 per night. Reservation deposit required. 460 RV sites (60-ft maximum RV length). 460 EWS. 50 amps. Disposal station. Flush toilets, cable TV and phone hookups. Heated pool, sauna, recreation room, sports court. Groceries. Coin laundry. Small pets only. AE, CB, DI, DS, MC, VI. (Private)

### BOULDER LAKES RV RESORT ⓦ √
*1 mi E of I-515/SR 93 and 95, exit Russell Rd, ¼ mi N at Desert Horizons Rd; 6201 Boulder Hwy, 89122.*
*(702) 435-1157; FAX (702) 435-1125.*
$19.50 per night for 2 persons. XP $2. Credit card guarantee; 3-day refund notice. Weekly and monthly rates available. 417 RV sites (50-ft maximum RV length). 417 EWS. Desert atmosphere, paved roads and pads. Flush toilets, cable TV and phone hookups. 4 pools, saunas, whirlpools, recreation room. Groceries. Coin laundry. No pets. MC, VI. (Private)

### CIRCUSLAND RV PARK √
*2⅓ mi S on the Strip, adjacent to Circus Circus Hotel; 500 Circus Circus Dr, 89109.*
*(702) 794-3757; FAX (702) 792-2280.*
Fri-Sat $18 per night, Sun-Thu $16 per night. Reservation deposit required. 35 acres. 364 RV sites. 384 EWS. All paved sites; many pull-thru. Disposal station, flush toilets. Pool, wading pool, sauna, whirlpool, playground. Groceries. Coin laundry. Pets. AE, DS, MC, VI. (Private)

### LAS VEGAS RESORT KOA √
*4 mi SE on US 93 and 95, just S of Desert Inn Rd; 4315 Boulder Hwy, 89121.*
*(702) 451-5527; FAX (702) 434-8729.*
$23.95-27.95 per night for 2 persons; XP $3-5. Credit card guarantee. 240 RV sites, many pull-thru; 60 tent sites. 240 EW, 180 S. Disposal station, flush toilets. Air conditioning or electric heater, $3. Heated pool, wading pool, whirlpool open 5/15-9/15. Playground, recreation

*Katherine Landing, on Lake Mohave, has full marina services in
addition to camping facilities.*

room, sports court. Self-service RV and car wash. Area transportation to Strip. Groceries,
propane. Coin laundry. Pets. DS, MC, VI. (Private)

### OASIS LAS VEGAS RV RESORT √
*Exit I-15 at Blue Diamond Rd (Exit 33), ½ mi E to Las Vegas Bl, ½ mi S to 2711 W Windmill,
89123.*
*(702) 260-2020; FAX (702) 263-5160.*
Fri-Sat $19-25 per night, Sun-Thu $16-21 per night. 14-night stay limit. Credit card guarantee. 702 RV sites. 702 EWS. Some pull-thru sites. Attractive grounds and facilities. Disposal
station, lounge, flush toilets. 2 pools, whirlpool, recreation room, fully equipped exercise facility, 18-hole putting course on natural turf greens. Groceries, propane. Coin laundry. Small pets
only. MC, VI. (Private)

### SAM'S TOWN RV PARKS ⓐⓐ √
*1 mi E of I-515/US 93 and 95, Flamingo exit; 5225 Boulder Hwy, 89122.*
*(702) 454-8055.*
$16-18 per night. 14-night stay limit. No tents allowed. Credit card guarantee. 500 RV sites. 500
EW, 476 S. Some pull-thru sites. Attractive grounds and facilities. Disposal station, flush toilets. 2
pools, whirlpools, recreation room. Coin laundry. Pets. AE, CB, DI, DS, MC, VI. (Private)

### SUNRISE RESORT & RV PARK ⓐⓐ √
*4995 Boulder Hwy, 89121.*
*(702) 458-7275; FAX (702) 898-7275.*
$17 per night. Reservation deposit required. 240 RV sites. 240 EWS. Flush toilets, 50 amps,
phone and cable TV hookups. Heated pool, whirlpool, recreation room, putting green.
Groceries, propane. Coin laundry. Pets, $25 deposit required. AE, DS, MC, VI. (Private)

# Primm

**PRIMADONNA RV VILLAGE** ⚌ √
*E of I-15, Primm exit, 45 mi S of Las Vegas; Box 19119, Primm 89019.*
*(702) 382-1212; FAX (702) 679-5494.*

$12 per night. 14-night stay limit. Reservations. 200 tent/RV sites. 200 EWS. Most sites pull-thru. Disposal station, piped water, flush toilets, cable TV hookups. Pool, whirlpool, playground, recreation room, sports court. Area transportation to casino. Groceries, propane. Coin laundry. Pets. AE, DI, DS, MC, VI. (Private)

# Red Rock Canyon National Conservation Area

**HEADQUARTERS** *18 mi W of the Strip via SR 159/W Charleston Bl; c/o Bureau of Land Management, Red Rock Canyon Visitor Center, HCR-33 Box 5500, Las Vegas, 89124.*
*(702) 363-1921.*

**Oak Creek** √ *Just S of BLM visitor center and Scenic Loop Dr on SR 159/W Charleston Bl; 4765 W Vegas Dr, 89108. (This campground is scheduled to be moved to n new location within the park during 1998. Contact the visitor center for further information.)*
$10 per night. Reservations not accepted. El 3600. 22 tent sites. 22 W. Primitive toilets, no showers. Visitor center. Pets, $3. (BLM)

# Spring Mountains National Recreation Area

**HEADQUARTERS** *35 mi NW of Las Vegas within the Humboldt-Toiyabe National Forest via US 95, turn off at SR 157/Kyle Canyon Rd or SR 156/Lee Canyon Rd. (702) 873-8800.*

*RV camping facilities in Las Vegas generally feature swimming pools, recreation rooms and convenient access to casino entertainment.*

*Campgrounds may open as early as mid-May and close as late as early Oct, depending on weather. For campsite reservations, call the National Forest Reservation Center at (800) 280-2267.*

**Dolomite** √ *29 mi NW on US 95, 18 mi SW on SR 156, 89018.*
$10 for family; $4 per additional vehicle. 14-night stay limit. Reservations. El 8400. 31 tent/RV sites (32-ft maximum RV length). Piped water, flush and primitive toilets, barbecues, fire rings, picnic tables, no showers. Nature trails. Pets. (NF)

**Fletcher View** √ *15 mi NW on US 95, 18 mi W on SR 157, 89018.*
$10 for family; $4 per additional vehicle. 14-night stay limit. No reservations. El 7200. 11 tent/RV sites (22-ft maximum RV length). Piped water, primitive toilets, barbecues, fire rings, some picnic tables, no showers. Riding stable within 1 mile. (NF)

**Hilltop** √ *15 mi NW on US 95, 17 mi W on SR 157, 6 mi NW on SR 158, 89018.*
$10 per night for family; $20 per night for multifamily site. 14-night stay limit. Reservations. El 8400. 31 tent/RV sites (maximum RV length varies). Piped water, flush toilets, coin-operated showers, barbecues, fire rings, picnic tables. Nature trails. 2 units are wheelchair accessible. (NF)

**Kyle Canyon** √ *15 mi NW on US 95, 17½ mi W on SR 157, 89018.*
$10 per night for family; $20 per night for multifamily site. 14-night stay limit. Reservations. El 7000. 25 tent/RV sites (32-ft maximum RV length). Piped water, primitive toilets, barbecues, fire rings, picnic tables, no showers. Riding stable within 1 mile. 9 units are wheelchair accessible. (NF)

**McWilliams** √ *29 mi NW on US 95; 18 mi SW on SR 156.*
$10 per night for family; $20 per night for multifamily site. 14-night stay limit. Reservations. El 8400. 40 tent/RV sites (32-ft maximum RV length). Piped water, flush and primitive toilets, barbecues, fire rings, picnic tables, no showers. (NF)

# Valley of Fire State Park

**HEADQUARTERS** *50 mi NE of Las Vegas via I-15 and SR 169; Box 515, Overton, 89040.* *(702) 397-2088.*

**Valley of Fire Campgrounds** √ *There are 2 campgrounds in the park located less than ½ mi apart.*
$11 per night. Reservations not accepted. 49 sites total. Piped water, flush and primitive toilets, showers, barbecues, fire rings, picnic tables. Nature trail. Visitor center. Pets. 2 sites are wheelchair accessible. (State)

# Bullhead City, Arizona

**MOHAVE COUNTY PARKS-DAVIS CAMP** √
*1 mi N on SR 95, below Davis Dam, 86430.*
*(520) 754-4606.*
$8-15 per night. 14-night stay limit on beach. Reservations not accepted. El 520. 171 RV sites (50-ft maximum RV length). 171 E, 141 WS. On Colorado River. Disposal station, piped water, flush toilets, showers, barbecues, fire rings. Boat ramp, dock; swimming, boating, fishing, playground. Propane, groceries within 5 miles. Coin laundry. Pets; dogs $1 per day. Wheelchair accessible. MC, VI. (County)

**SNOWBIRD RV RESORT** √
*8 mi S on SR 95, just E on Joy Ln, 1600 Joy Ln, 86426.*
*(520) 768-7141.*
$16 per night for 2 persons. XP $3. Reservation deposit required; credit cards not accepted. 10 tent, 125 RV sites. 125 EWS, 50 amps. Disposal station, piped water, flush toilets. Cable TV and phone hookups; 9-hole golf course, complimentary to guests. Heated pool, whirlpool; playground, recreation room. Coin laundry. Pets. Wheelchair accessible. (Private)

# Index

This index contains listings for points of interest, recreational activities, events and services.

# Index to Advertisers

For information about placing an advertisement in
Automobile Club of Southern California publications, please contact:

**Alisa Fouse** or **Karen Clyne**
Advertising Services, A327
Automobile Club of Southern California
3333 Fairview Road
Costa Mesa, CA 92626
(714) 885-2375; FAX (714) 885-2335

# Acknowledgements

| | |
|---|---|
| **Writer** | David J. Brackney |
| **Cartographer** | Andrew M. Gordon |
| **Graphic Artist** | Michael C. Lee |
| **Editor** | Kristine Miller |

## Photography

| | |
|---|---|
| 6, 15 (archive), 38, 49, 54, 55, 57, 71, 77 (dam), 89, 94, 101 | **Las Vegas News Bureau** |
| (Cover), 5, 34, 36, 39 (Lied Museum), 42, 46, 65, 70, 96 | **Todd Masinter** |
| 9, 15 (petroglyphs), 16, 41, 50, 59, 66, 77 (dock), 93 | **David J. Brackney** |
| 13, 26, 63, 70, 82, 83 | **Robert Brown** |
| 11, 68, 135 | **Chris Hart** |
| 136 | **Circus Circus Hotel** |
| 27 | **Ethel M Chocolates Factory** |
| 52 | **Excalibur Hotel & Casino** |
| 51 | **Flamingo Hilton** |
| 21 | **Las Vegas Wedding Coordinators** |
| 39 (pianos) | **Liberace Museum** |
| 102 | **McCarran International Airport** |
| 43 | **Scandia Family Fun Center** |
| 45 | **Wet 'n Wild** |
| 10 | **World of Coca-Cola Las Vegas** |